Revising
Business
Prose

RICHARD A. LANHAM

UNIVERSITY OF CALIFORNIA, LOS ANGELES
PRESIDENT, RHETORICA, INC.

Revising Business Prose

Second Edition

MACMILLAN PUBLISHING COMPANY
NEW YORK
COLLIER MACMILLAN PUBLISHERS
LONDON

Earlier edition copyright © 1981 by Richard A. Lanham,
published by Charles Scribner's Sons.

Portions of this work appear in modified form in
Revising Prose, Second Edition, Copyright © 1987 by Richard A. Lanham.

Macmillan Publishing Company
866 Third Avenue, New York, New York 10022

Collier Macmillan Canada, Inc.

Library of Congress Cataloging-in-Publication Data

Lanham, Richard A.
  Revising business prose.

  1. English language—Business English. 2. English
language—Style. 3. English language—Rhetoric.
4. Editing. I. Title.
PE1479.B87L36 1987   808'.066651   86-12691
ISBN 0-02-367430-X

Printing: 5 6 7   Year: 9 0 1 2 3

ISBN 0-02-367430-X

Preface

What should written communication in business be like? It ought to be fast, specific, and responsible. It should show someone acting, doing something to or for someone else. Business life offers few occasions for the descriptive set-piece. It chronicles history in the making, depicts someone acting on matter or on people. Abstractions occur in an applied context, form part of a problem. Business prose ought to be verb-style prose, lining up actor, action, and object in a chain of power and lining them up fast.

Increasingly, though, it is moving in just the opposite direction, toward a special language we might call the "Official Style." The Official Style is the language of bureaucracies, of large organizations; it is a noun-centered language, abstract, voiced always in the passive, and slow. Above all, it strives to disguise the actor, allow such action as cannot be quashed entirely to seep out in an impersonal construction—never "I decided" but always "It has been decided that. . . ."

It isn't hard to see why the Official Style threatens to inherit the business world as it has done the government. We are all bureaucrats these days, or shortly will be, whether we work for the government directly or work in the private sector and get our government money through grants, contracts, or subsidies. And even if—especially if—we belong to that shrinking part of the private sector that remains really private, we'll be for certain filling out government forms, having OSHA for lunch whether we invited her or not.

Thus we all have to do business in the Official Style—Federalese, Bureaucratese, Sociologese, Educationese, Doublespeak, or only our firm's "company style." And to do business in it, we will often—though not always—want to translate it into English. If "initiation of the termination process is now considered appropriate" *re* us, we have to know that it's time to be looking for another job. And some of us may also practice this kind of translation in the name of business efficiency, verbal aesthetics, or plain cultural sanity.

People think this "plague" of bureaucratic writing is hard to cure. Not so. Nothing is easier—if you want to cure it. The Paramedic Method suggested here provides just the emergency therapy needed—a quick, self-teaching method of revision for people who want to translate the Official Style, their own or someone else's, into plain English. But it is just that—a first aid kit. It's not the art of medicine. As with paramedicine in underdeveloped countries, it does not attempt to teach a full body of knowledge but only to diagnose and cure the epidemic disease. It won't answer, though at the end it addresses, the big question: having the cure, how do you know when, or if, you should take it? For this you need the art of medicine, and for prose style this means a mature training in verbal self-awareness, coupled with wide reading and continued writing. The second edition of *Revising Business Prose* offers something considerably less ambitious, not a liberal education or even a businesslike Muse, but only a specific method for a specific problem.

We'll begin with some nuts-and-bolts details of sentence shape, rhythm, and emphasis, and then try to focus the Official Style as a whole, ask what it is and does and why it came about. Next, we'll work through a case study that shows the perils of prose revision in a bureaucratic context like that in which so many of us work. Finally, we'll consider briefly the central question—when to use the Official Style and when to leave it alone. And, as a concluding note, I'll glance at the electronic revolution now sweeping over business communication of all sorts.

I'm trying to make you hyperconscious about the Official Style. After all, you can't hit what you can't see. Since people no longer seem to know much grammar, I've included the basic terms in an Appendix. All the prose examples, by the way—the "Jim kicks Bill" paradigm excepted—come from real writing in what, with some exaggeration, we call "the real world."

A word on the Paramedic Method—(PM). It works only if you *follow* it rather than *argue* with it. When it tells you to get rid of the prepositional phrases, get rid of them. Don't go into a "but, well, in this case, given my style, really I need to . . ." bob and weave. You'll never learn anything that way. The PM constitutes the center of this book. Use it. It's printed in full on page xii; clip it out and tack it above your desk for easy reference.

R. A. L.

Note: A half-hour video cassette, also called *Revising Business Prose,* is available for use with this book. Through digital videographics, it shows the Paramedic Method at work in color and sound.

Contents

Contents

Revising
Business
Prose

The Paramedic Method

1. Circle the prepositions.
2. Circle the "is" forms.
3. Ask "Who is kicking who?"
4. Put this "kicking" action in a simple (not compound) active verb.
5. Start fast—no mindless introductions.
6. Write out each sentence on a blank sheet of paper and mark off its basic rhythmic units with a "/".
7. Read the passage aloud with emphasis and feeling.
8. Mark off sentence lengths in the passage with a "/".

CHAPTER 1

Who's Kicking Who?

No responsible business person these days would feel comfortable writing simply "Jim kicks Bill." The system seems to require something like "One can easily see that a kicking situation is being implemented between Bill and Jim." Or, "This is the kind of situation in which Jim is a kicker and Bill is a kickee." Jim cannot enjoy kicking Bill; no, for official use, it must be "Kicking Bill is an ongoing activity hugely enjoyed by Jim." Absurdly contrived examples? Here are some real ones:

This office is in need of a dynamic manager of sales.

After reviewing the research and in light of the relevant information found within the context of the conclusions, we feel that there is definite need for some additional research to more specifically pinpoint our advertising and marketing strategies.

Ms. Jones is attempting to reduce the number of personnel attending meetings with the goal of sending only one representative to any given meeting. If decisions are expected to result from the meeting, the cognizant decision maker attends the meeting. This eliminates the requirement to further recommunicate facts necessary for making the decision.

See what they have in common? They are like our Bill and Jim examples, assembled from strings of prepositional phrases glued together by that all-purpose epoxy "is." In each case the sentence's verbal force has been shunted into a noun and for a verb we make do with "is," the neutral copulative, the weakest verb in the language. Such sentences project no life, no vigor. They just "are." And the "is" generates those strings of prepositional phrases fore and aft. It's so easy to fix. Look for the real action. Ask yourself, who's kicking who? (Yes, I know, it should be *whom,* but doesn't it sound stilted?)

In "This office is in need of a dynamic manager of sales," the action obviously lies in "need." And so, "This office needs a dynamic sales manager." The needless prepositional phrase, "in need of," simply disappears once we see who's kicking who. The sentence, animated by a real verb, comes alive, and in seven words instead of eleven. (If you've not paid attention to your own writing before, think of a lard factor [LF] of one-third to one-half as normal and don't stop revising until you've removed it.) The lard factor is found by dividing the difference between the number of words in the original and the revision by the number of words in the original—in this case:

$$11 - 7 = 4 \div 11 = 0.36 \text{ or } 36\%$$

We now have the beginnings of the Paramedic Method (PM):

1. Circle the prepositions.
2. Circle the "is" forms.
3. Ask "Who is kicking who?"
4. Put this "kicking" action in a simple (not compound) active verb.

What about the second example?

After reviewing the research and in light of the relevant information found within the context of the conclusions, we feel that there is definite need for some additional research to more specifically pinpoint our advertising and marketing strategies.

The standard formula: "is" + prepositional phrases fore and aft. Who's kicking who here? Well, the kicker is obviously "we." And the action? "Needing," just as in the previous example, and here buried in "there is definite need for." So the core of the sentence emerges as "We need more research." Let's revise what comes before and after this central statement.

After reviewing the research and in light of the relevant information found within the context of the conclusions, we feel that there is definite need for some additional research to more specifically pinpoint our advertising and marketing strategies.

[handwritten annotations: "of previous", "suggest that", "more"]

The completed revision then reads:

The conclusions of previous research suggest that we need more research to pinpoint our advertising and marketing strategies.

Eighteen words instead of 38—LF 53%. Not bad—but wait a minute. How about "the conclusions of"? Do we really need it? Why not just:

Previous research suggests that we need more research to pinpoint our advertising and marketing strategies. (LF 60%)

And this revision, as so often happens, suggests a further and more daring one:

3

has failed

Previous research ~~suggests that we need more research~~ to pinpoint our advertising and marketing strategies. (LF 71%)

By now, of course, we've changed kicker and kickee and, to an extent, the meaning. But isn't the new meaning what the writer really wanted to say in the first place? A previous failure has generated a subsequent need? And the new version *sounds* better, too. The awkward repetition of "research" has been avoided and we've finally found the real first kicker, "Previous research," and found out what it was doing—it "failed." We can now bring in the second kicker in an emphatic second sentence:

> Previous research has failed to pinpoint our advertising and marketing strategies. *We need to know more.*

No "is," no prepositional phrases, an LF of 58%, and the two actors and actions clearly sorted out.

The drill for this problem stands clear. Circle every form of "to be" (e.g., "is," "was," "will be," "seems to be") and every prepositional phrase. Then find out who's kicking who and start rebuilding the sentence with that action. Two prepositional phrases in a row turn on the warning light, three make a problem, and four invite disaster.

With a little practice, sentences like

> The role of markets is easily observed and understood when dealing with a simple commodity such as potatoes.

will turn into

> Examining a simple commodity like potatoes shows clearly how markets work. (LF 39%)

You will see more quickly how to infuse our third example

with some life and vigor. The opening sentence shows the typical "is" plus-prepositional-phrases form:

Ms. Jones *is attempting*
   to reduce the number
   of personnel attending meetings
   with the goal
   of sending only one representative
   to any given meeting.

I've cheated a little by putting the infinitive phrase "to reduce" in the prepositional phrase list, but here, as so often, it works structurally in just the same way as the prepositional phrases, making the sentence look and read like a laundry list. Try reading it aloud. Hear the list-like monotony? What can we do to break up this pattern?

First, substitute a single emphatic verb for the compound "is attempting." "Ms. Jones *wants* . . ." The next element— "to reduce the number of personnel attending meetings with the goal of sending only one representative"—says the same thing twice. Once is enough: "Ms. Jones wants to send only one person to each meeting." We have reduced 23 words to 11, made the sentence half as long and twice as clear. The second sentence needs an active verb insted of a passive one; when you supply it, you see a form waiting to emerge:

ORIGINAL

If decisions are expected to result from the meeting, the cognizant decision maker attends the meeting.

REVISION

If the meeting is going to make decisions, the decision maker should attend.

Usually, you can collapse "is going to make decisions" into "decide something," and thus satisfy the PM rule that asks for a simple rather than a compound verb—"decide" rather than "make decisions." But here I am trying to let a classical verbal shape emerge, one called *chiasmus,* in which an initial A:B sequence is matched later, for symmetry and balance, by a B:A sequence: "make decisions" and "decision-maker." Chiasmus draws the two elements of the sentence together into a tighter structure, yokes the verb phrase ("makes decisions") and the noun ("decision-maker") together. Shapes like these are fun to see and read because the shape and sound reinforce the meaning, and make the sentence easier to understand by drawing the related elements more closely together.

And what of the third sentence? You could add it to the second: "If the meeting is going to make decisions, the decision maker should attend herself, and not hear about it secondhand." But do you really need the third sentence at all? Isn't it implied by the second? Doesn't this writer, as we saw in the first sentence, spell things out too much? I think we can eliminate it. And so we have:

ORIGINAL

Ms. Jones is attempting to reduce the number of personnel attending meetings with the goal of sending only one representative to any given meeting. If decisions are expected to result from the meeting, the cognizant decision maker attends the meeting. This eliminates the requirement to further recommunicate facts necessary for making the decision.

REVISION

Ms. Jones wants to send only one person to each meeting. If the meeting is going to make decisions, the decision maker attends.

We have reduced 53 words to 23, a lard factor of 57%. And it is much more than twice as clear. The "Official Style" is not only long-winded; it is hard to read.

The Official Style can be found in all kinds of writing.

Look at these "of" strings from a communications theorist, a literary critic, and a popular gourmet:

It is the totality *of* the interrelation *of* the various components *of* language and the other communication systems which is the basis for referential memory.

These examples *of* unusual appropriateness *of* the sense *of* adequacy to the situation suggest the primary signification *of* rhyme in the usual run *of* lyric poetry.

Frozen breads and frozen pastry completed the process *of* depriving the American woman *of* the pleasure *of* boasting *of* her baking.

These "of" strings are the worst. They remind you of a child pulling a gob of bubble gum out into a long string. When you try to revise them, you can feel how fatally easy the "is and of" formulation can be for expository prose. And how fatally confusing, too, since to find an active, transitive verb for "is" means, often, adding a specificity the writer has not provided. So, in the first example, what does "is the basis for" really mean? And does the writer mean that language's components interact with "other communication systems," or is he talking about "components" of "other communication systems" as well? The "of" phrases refer back to those going before in so general a way that you can't keep straight what really modifies what. So revision here, alas, is partly a guess.

ORIGINAL

It is the totality of the interrelation of the various components of language and the other communication systems which is the basis for referential meaning.

REVISION 1

Referential meaning emerges when the components of language interact with other communication systems.

7

Or the sentence might mean:

REVISION 2

Referential meaning emerges when the components of language interact with the components of other communications systems.

Do you see the writer's problem? He has tried to be more specific than he needs to be, to build his sentence on a noun ("totality") that demands a string of "of's" to qualify it. Ask where the action is, build the sentence on a *verb*, and the "totality" follows as an implication.

The second example shows even more clearly how an "of" string can blur what goes with what. Do the first two prepositional phrases ("of the sense of adequacy") form a unit that refers back to "appropriateness"? That is, something like this:

of the sense of adequacy

These examples of unusual appropriateness to the situation

suggest . . .

Or are we to take all three prepositional phrases as a subunit that refers back to "appropriateness"? Something like this:

of the sense of adequacy to the situation

These examples of unusual appropriateness suggest . . .

No way to tell, and the irresolution between the two blurs our vision. Taking such a sentence out of context doesn't help, of course, but even in context we'd stop and blink to clear our eyes. Here's the original again and my best guess for a revision:

ORIGINAL

These examples of unusual appropriateness of the sense of adequacy to the situation suggest the primary signification of rhyme in the usual run of lyrical poetry.

REVISION

These examples, where adequacy to the situation seems unusually appropriate, suggest how rhyme usually works in lyric poetry.

The third passage is much easier to fix:

ORIGINAL

Frozen breads and frozen pastry completed the process of depriving the American woman of the pleasure of boasting of her baking.

REVISION

No longer, after frozen breads and pastry, could the American woman boast about her baking.

In asking who's kicking who, a couple of mechanical tricks come in handy. Besides getting rid of the "is's" and changing every passive voice ("is defended by") to an active voice ("defends"), you can squeeze the compound verbs hard, make every "are able to" turn into a "can," every "seems to succeed in creating" into "creates," every "cognize the fact that" (no, I didn't make it up) into "think," every "am hopeful that" into "hope," every "provides us with an example of" into "exemplifies," every "seeks to reveal" into "shows," and every "there is the inclusion of" into "includes."

And you can amputate those mindless introductory phrases, "The fact of the matter is that" and "The nature of the case is that." Start fast and then, as they say in the movies, "Cut to the chase." Instead of "The answer is in the negative," you'll find yourself saying "No."

We now can add a rule to the Paramedic Method (PM):

1. Circle the prepositions.
2. Circle the "is" forms.
3. Ask "Who is kicking who?"

9

4. Put this "kicking" action in a simple (not compound) active verb.

5. Start fast—no mindless introductions.

Let's try out this PM on some samples of the Official Style. We want plain language nonfat versions half as long and with some zip.

The Official Style is often used to cover up things you'd rather not say at all. One of Ted Kennedy's aides, for example, was asked if the race against Jimmy Carter for the 1980 Democratic nomination was proving harder than expected. He couldn't give a straight "yes" or "no" answer—*nobody* in Washington does that—and so translated the question into the Official Style:

The intellectual appreciation of the difficulty was not up to the reality.

I've done steps 1 and 2 of the PM. For rule #3—who's kicking who—we have to add a kicker, a *person* performing an *act,* since none is provided: "The intellectual appreciation was not up to" = "We didn't *understand.*" For the kickee, add "how hard it would actually be" = "We didn't understand how hard it would actually be." We've complied with rule #4—simple verb form—and rule #5, too—start fast. Notice how slow off the mark the original is? Six words before you get to a verb and then only a lifeless "was."

Now, in a slightly longer passage, we move to advertising. Read the passage over and sketch out for yourself how the revision should proceed. Then we'll work through it sentence by sentence.

The first project that should be undertaken should obtain a measure of the acceptability of the product's *taste* and *usage.* If the majority of the consumers express dissatisfaction with the product's taste, then attempts to establish the current product are doomed. Product taste and usage are especially critical for the sweetener. If there is significant negative reaction to the taste, then changes in the recipe would be recommended. If there was confusion about the suitability of granulated flavoring for use as a topping or spread, then one of the major goals of advertising would be to educate the public on the product's use. Research on consumer reaction to the product is essential to answer several of the basic questions about how to best market this new product.

We can fix the first sentence by simple subtraction:

The first project ~~that should be undertaken~~ should ~~obtain a~~ measure ~~of~~ the acceptability of the product's taste and usage.

Kicker: "first project"; action: "measure"; kickee: "acceptability" (LF 30%). The revision now reads:

The first project should measure the acceptability of the product's *taste* and *usage*.

The second sentence requires more work:

If the majority of the consumers express dissatisfaction with the product's taste, then attempts to establish the current product are doomed.

Not an egregious example of the Official Style, this, but dead, lifeless. It couldn't inspire anyone to sell anything. It takes too long to get going and it ends with no emphasis, no zip. The trouble, as always, lies in the verbs—"express dissatisfaction" and "are doomed." How about this revision?

If consumers don't like the product's taste, it won't sell.

11

"The majority of" provides a needless specification that slows down the sentence's opening; "Express dissatisfaction with" is a prissy way of saying "don't like"; "then attempts to establish the current product are doomed" is a long-winded way to say "it won't sell." Notice how this windiness drains all the life from the last half of the sentence? And, now that we've gotten this far, the obvious final revision presents itself: "If the product tastes bad, it won't sell."

The rest of the passage offers the basic Official Style pattern—"is" + prepositional phrases—almost entirely. For verb choice, with the exception of one construction—"would be recommended"—only "is" gets the nod. I'll circle the prepositions and the "is" forms.

Product taste and usage (are) especially critical (for) the sweetener. If there (is) significant negative reaction (to) the taste, then changes (in) the recipe (would be) recommended. If there (was) confusion (about) the suitability (of) granulated flavoring (for) use (as) a topping or spread, then one (of) the major goals (of) advertising (would be) to educate the public (on) the product's use. Research (on) consumer reaction (to) the product (is) essential to answer several (of) the basic questions (about) how best to market this new product.

In the revisions that follow, I'm obeying rules 3–5, asking who's kicking who, putting that action in a simple verb, and starting the sentence fast.

ORIGINAL

Product taste and usage are especially critical for the sweetener.

Here's a classic case of blurring the action. The sentence seems to say that "Product taste and usage" are doing something to "the sweetener" when actually, as the passage goes on to explain, it works just the other way around. The sweetener determines how the product tastes and is used. Why not just say so?

> The sweetener determines how the product tastes and is used.

The other revisions follow easily, once we have this basic argument clear:

If ~~there is significant reaction to the~~ taste, ~~then changes in the recipe would be recommended~~. If ~~there was confusion about the suitability of~~ granulated flavoring ~~for use~~ as a topping or spread, then ~~one of the major goals of advertising would be to educate the public on the product's use~~.
Research on consumer reaction ~~to the product is essential to~~ answer ~~several of the~~ basic questions ~~about how~~ to ~~best~~

people don't like its (taste) *we should change it.* *they don't know how to use* (granulated flavoring) *our advertising must show them.* *must* (reaction) *these* (questions) *if we are* to

market this new product.

So the whole revision looks like this:

ORIGINAL

The first project that should be undertaken should obtain a measure of the acceptability of the product's *taste* and *usage*. If the majority of the consumers express dissatisfaction with the product's taste, then attempts to establish the current product are doomed. Product taste and usage are especially critical for the sweetener. If there is significant negative reaction to the taste, then changes in the recipe would be recommended. If there was confusion about the suitability of granulated flavoring for use as a topping or spread, then one of the major goals of advertising would be to educate the public on the product's use. Research on

13

consumer reaction to the product is essential to answer several of the basic questions about how to best market this new product.

REVISION

The first project should measure the acceptability of the product's *taste* and *usage*. If consumers don't like the product's taste, it won't sell. The sweetener determines how the product tastes and is used. If people don't like its taste, we should change it. If they don't know how to use granulated flavoring as a topping or spread, then our advertising must show them. Research on consumer reaction must answer these basic questions if we are to market this new product.

Thus de-larded, the passage suggests a further revision: we don't really need the last sentence at all, since it is implied by the first. Just add a "research" before the third word, "project." No need to talk about selling the product as the goal of all this—that's the name of the game.

So the original and final revision look like this:

ORIGINAL

The first project that should be undertaken should obtain a measure of the acceptability of the product's *taste* and *usage*. If the majority of the consumers express dissatisfaction with the product's taste, then attempts to establish the current product are doomed. Product taste and usage are especially critical for the sweetener. If there is significant negative reaction to the taste, then changes in the recipe would be recommended. If there was confusion about the suitability of granulated flavoring for use as a topping or spread, then one of the major goals of advertising would be to educate the public on the product's use. Research on consumer reaction to the product is essential to answer several of the basic questions about how to best market this new product.

REVISION

The first research project should measure the acceptability of the product's *taste* and *usage*. If the product tastes bad, it won't sell. The sweetener determines how the product tastes and is used. If people don't like its taste, we should change it. If they don't know how to use granulated flavoring as a topping or spread, then advertising must show them. (63 words instead of 127; LF 50%)

Yes, of course this kind of revision is tedious and time consuming. But, using the PM, you'll soon get good at doing it quickly. Isn't getting on with your business twice as fast worth the effort? And in working, as in the rest of life, it's a big help to know where the action is, who's really kicking who. Again, the PM rules thus far:

1. Circle the prepositions.
2. Circle the "is" forms.
3. Ask "Who is kicking who?"
4. Put this "kicking" action in a simple (not compound) active verb.
5. Start fast—no mindless introductions.

CHAPTER 2

Sentences and Shopping Bags

None of the sentences you've just worked through has any shape. They just go on and on, as if they were emerging from a nonstop sausage machine. This shapelessness makes them unreadable: you cannot read them aloud with expressive emphasis. Try to. When language as spoken and heard has completely atrophied, the sentence becomes less a shaped unit of emphatic utterance than a shopping bag of words. Read your own prose aloud and with emphasis—or better still, have a friend read it to you. This rehearsal can often tell you more about failures of shape, rhythm, and emphasis of your sentences than any other single device. You might try, too, writing a single sentence on a sheet of blank paper. Forget meaning for a minute and just look at the sentence's shape. Try to isolate the basic parts and trace their relationship to one another. Looking for the natural shape of a sentence often suggests the quickest way to revision.

When prose is read aloud, the voice can shape and punctuate as it goes along. But when the voice atrophies, the eye does not make the same demands with equal insistence, and the larger shaping rhythms that build through a paragraph tend to blur. A problem hard to see and hard to remedy. Consider this passage from a recent popular article by an American economist, which shows the type of prose business people have to read all the time:

A third advantage of the market as a means of social organization is its "devil-take-the-hindmost" approach to questions of individual equity. At first blush this is an outrageous statement worthy of the coldest heart among the nineteenth-century Benthamites. And obviously I have stated the point in a way more designed to catch the eye than to be precise.

In any except a completely stagnant society, an efficient use of resources requires constant change. Consumer tastes, production technologies, locational advantages, and resource availabilities are always in flux. From the standpoint of static efficiency, the more completely and rapidly the economy shifts production to meet changes in tastes, resource availability or locational advantages, the greater the efficiency. From a dynamic standpoint, the greater the advances in technology and the faster they're adopted, the greater the efficiency. While these changes on balance generate gains for society in the form of higher living standards, almost every one of them causes a loss of income to some firms and individuals, often temporary and for only a few, but sometimes long-lasting and for large numbers.

What do you notice? Well, that first sentence, for a start— an almost perfect Normative Official Sentence, though now from a high government official:

A third advantage
   of the market
   as a means
   of social organization
is its "devil-take-the-hindmost" approach
   to questions
   of individual equity.

Although the sentences do not run to an exact length, they are mostly long and monotonous. No short sentences means no

large-scale emphasis, no climax and finality. The last sentence
of paragraph one, though much shorter than any other,
doesn't summarize anything. How to supply some shape? For
a start, get the lard out of the first paragraph:

A third advantage ~~of~~ the market's as a ~~means of~~ social
organization ~~is~~ rests in its "devil-take-the-hindmost" approach to
~~questions of~~ individual equity. At first blush this ~~is an~~
outrageous statement seems worthy of the coldest heart ~~among~~
~~the nineteenth-century~~ Benthamite. And obviously I have
stated the point ~~in a way more designed~~ to catch the eye.
~~than to be precise.~~

What has been done? I've made one assumption the writer
did not, that the audience knows "Benthamite" implies
"nineteenth century." Otherwise, only fat has been removed.
The rhythm has picked up a little. The first sentence now
begins more quickly and it has a real verb (though "rests"
may not be ideal—how about "remains" or "stands"?).
Phrases such as "questions of," "problems of," and "factors
of" are simply mindless fillers, bad habits like saying "like"
and "you know" after every third word. A plain noun, left by
itself, often comes across stronger. The changes in the second
sentence all aim to increase the emphasis on "outrageous
statement." In the third, I've tried to underscore the parallelism of "stated the point" and "catch the eye."

The original and revision so far:

ORIGINAL

A third advantage of the market as a means of social
organization is its "devil-take-the-hindmost" approach to
questions of individual equity. At first blush this is an
outrageous statement worthy of the coldest heart among

19

the nineteenth-century Benthamites. And obviously I have stated the point in a way more designed to catch the eye than to be precise.

REVISION

The market's third advantage as a social organization rests in its "devil-take-the-hindmost" approach to individual equity. This outrageous statement seems, at first blush, worthy of the coldest Benthamite heart. And obviously I have stated the point to catch the eye. (LF 33%)

Sentence lengths of 19–13–11 instead of 24–18–20. The result may still fall short of greatness, but at least a decreasing length pattern has begun to form and the last sentence has a bit of zip. Sometimes little changes take you a long way:

In any except a ~~completely~~ stagnant society, ~~an~~ efficient use of resources requires constant change.

Again, the adverbial intensifier ("completely") weakens instead of strengthens. And we want to reach "stagnant society" more quickly. Read the two versions aloud several times. Does the revision succeed in placing more stress on "constant change"? The same desire for end-stress now changes "are always in flux" to "always change" in the next sentence. In the following one:

~~From the standpoint of~~ For static efficiency, the more ~~completely and~~ rapidly the economy shifts production to meet changes in taste, resource availability, or locational advantages, the ~~greater the efficiency~~ better.

Now we want to preserve the static/dynamic contrast he is developing—"for static efficiency/for dynamic efficiency":

> ~~From~~ **For** a dynamic ~~standpoint~~, the ~~greater~~ **efficiency** the ~~advances in~~
> technolog~~y and the faster they are adopted~~ **ical changes** **faster**, the ~~greater the~~ **better.**
> ~~efficiency.~~

The two sentences still end with the same phrase, but because they connect more closely the prose no longer sounds like a list or catalogue.

The curse of the Official Style is spelling everything out. The Official Stylist prepares an assertion the way a cook prepares abalone, by beating it repeatedly with a hammer to make it tender. So in the previous sentence, and in the one that follows:

> While these changes ~~on balance~~ generate ~~gains for society~~
> ~~in the form of~~ higher living standards, almost ~~every one of~~
> ~~them causes a loss of~~ **all decrease** income, ~~to some firms and individ-~~
> ~~uals~~, often temporarily and for ~~only~~ a few, but sometimes
> ~~long-lasting~~ **permanently** and for ~~large numbers~~ **many**. (LF 50%)

The sense may require "on balance," but everything else removed is pure lard. Again, the revision stresses the ending parallelism:

> temporarily and for a few
> permanently and for many.

Our revision so far, then, reads like this:

> The market's third advantage as a social organization rests in its "devil-take-the-hindmost" approach to individual equity. This outrageous statement seems, at first blush, worthy of the coldest Benthamite heart. And obviously I have stated the point to catch the eye.

Except in a stagnant society, efficient use of resources requires constant change. For static efficiency, the more rapidly the economy shifts production to meet changing tastes, resources, or locations, the better. For dynamic efficiency, the faster the technological change, the better. While these changes generate higher living standards, almost all decrease income, often temporarily and for a few, but sometimes permanently and for many. (LF 42%)

Sometimes you can see sentence shape trying to emerge through the lard:

ORIGINAL

All that it really means is that more and more software will be developed faster and faster and that the software will be much more reliable and easier to maintain.

Here the basic shape stands out:

more and more
faster and faster
more reliable
easier to maintain.

"More and more" "faster and faster," and "easier." You always want to *build on* patterns such as this; give the eye and ear a shape that reinforces the meaning. Revision here is dead easy. The awkward and sluggish ("All that . . . is that") opening can simply be amputated, as can "that the software," yielding:

REVISION

More and more software will be developed faster and faster, and will be more reliable and easier to maintain.

We have saved a few words (19 instead of 30; LF 37%) but the great improvement lies in sentence shape. Faster to see, and easier to understand.

Shapeless prose has a hard time conveying strong feeling,

or emphasizing its point. The emotional power simply dribbles away into waterlogged sentences. Look at the following confession of an advertising person:

ORIGINAL

Financial influence of commercial sponsors have devalued the quality of prime time television. Educational and social value of the programs are of secondary importance, as long as the producers can achieve the ratings expected by broadcasters and sponsors.

Let me suggest a revision and then explain where I am trying to go with it.

REVISION

Commercial sponsors have ruined prime time television. They have sacrificed educational and social values to audience ratings.

First, I tried to find the *primary actor* in this drama, the "commercial sponsors," rather than their derivative, "financial influence." Second, I made this primary actor the subject in both sentences, to give them a parallel structure that you can see and hear. Third, I have used two strong active verbs, "ruined" and "sacrificed." The *action* in the sentence is strong, but the verbs the writer has chosen—"devalued" and "are of secondary importance"—generate no force. And the amount of sheer lard in the original sentence (17 words instead of 38; LF 63%) makes things even worse.

Punchless prose such as this projects a punchless, flabby, muddle-headed public self, the last thing a business person wants to do. You don't need a public demonstration that your mind needs six months at the local Nautilus. With such a caution in mind, look at this piece of everyday business prose:

ORIGINAL

On the basis of the answers to these and other questions which the team might ask, I would expect the team to present us with detailed recommendations for enhancing the effectiveness of our reporting. If the recommendations are approved, we would begin to implement them immediately upon completion of the project. I would welcome a team with a broad diversity of interests, including but not limited to human resource management. Because of the focus on reporting, I would especially welcome the participation of at least one individual with a strong interest in Finance or Accounting.

Nothing really serious here, no arm numbness or deep chest pain. Just flab, flab, flab, and its accompanying arhythmia. Needless repetition: "the team . . . the team." Strings of jaw-breaking tongue-twisters: "recommendations for enhancing the effectiveness." A kind of Spanish chorus of aye, aye, ayes: "I would expect . . . I would welcome . . . I would especially welcome." And all so easy to fix. Let me revise it in longhand:

Building on
~~On the basis of~~ the answers to these, ~~and other~~ questions *like* *should* ~~which~~ the team ~~might ask, I would expect the team to~~ *improvements in* ~~present us with detailed~~ recommend~~ations for enhancing~~ ~~the effectiveness of~~ our reporting. If the recommendations ~~are~~ approved, ~~we would~~ *be* implement~~em them~~ *ed* immediately ~~upon completion of the project.~~ I *want* ~~would welcome~~ a *especially in* team with ~~a~~ broad ~~diversity of~~ interests, ~~including but not~~ *and given* ~~limited to~~ human resource management, ~~Because of~~ the *focus* ~~on~~ reporting, ~~I would especially welcome the participation of at least one individual with a strong interest~~ in Finance or Accounting.

REVISION

Building on the answers to questions like these, the team should recommend improvements in our reporting. If approved, the recommendations would be implemented immediately. I want a team with broad interests, especially in human resource management and, given the reporting focus, in Finance or Accounting. (94 words to 45; LF 52%)

The great improvement here comes in the voice; crisper, clearer, faster, more emphatic. A voice in command.

Here is a passage from a book on marketing. The prose is not unclear, only lifeless, flat, boring to read. It gives your understanding no help.

> As is true of other markets, the most fruitful way of penetrating the financial markets analytically is to break the subject down into the supply and demand aspects. The problem of doing so in this case is that the same institutions may be supply elements at one time and in one circumstance but demand elements at other times and under differing circumstances. For example, business corporations are important elements in these markets and are usually on the borrowing side of both the money and capital markets. Nevertheless, most large corporations are also important lenders in the money markets.

Here, we need only subtract and rearrange, not gaze into a crystal ball:

As ~~is true~~ **with** of other markets, ~~the most fruitful way of penetrating the~~ **breaking down** financial markets ~~analytically is to break the subject down~~ into ~~the~~ supply and demand ~~aspects~~ **makes analysis easier.**

The revision puts the central assertion—making analysis easier—at the end of the sentence, where it receives a natural stress. And the revision gets the sentence going faster, too, tightening up the introductory phrase and introducing the important words—"breaking" and "financial markets"—sooner. Do you notice how meaningless fillers like "aspects" blur the words they are meant to sharpen?

25

~~The problem of doing so in this case is that~~ *But* the same
institutions may be supply elements at one time and ~~in one~~
circumstance ~~but~~ *and* demand elements at ~~other times and~~ *another.*
~~under differing circumstances.~~

Two things are remarkable here. Notice how long the sentence takes to get started? By the time this wind-up is over, we've all stolen second base, and maybe third too. And notice how the words we've excised from the second half of the sentence gave it only a pseudo-precision? They really qualified nothing. Even when the qualifications are genuine, you'll usually do better sacrificing them for a tighter rhythm such as, here, the nice balance of "A at one time; B at another." Often the extra detail offered will, as in this passage, turn out bogus anyway.

For example, ~~business~~ corporations, ~~are important ele-~~
~~ments in these markets and are~~ usually ~~on the borrowing~~ *borrowers in*
~~side of~~ both ~~the~~ money and capital markets, ~~Nevertheless,~~
~~most large corporations~~ are also important lenders in the
money markets.

Here the original has done just the wrong thing. The two antithetical elements, borrowers and lenders, should be kept close together to give the contrast some zing. Instead, they are sequestered into separate sentences. The revision, by correcting the damage, intensifies the comparison.

Corporations, for example, usually borrowers in both money and capital markets, are also important lenders in the money markets.

And so the whole passage looks like this:

26

ORIGINAL

As is true of other markets, the most fruitful way of penetrating the financial markets analytically is to break the subject down into the supply and demand aspects. The problem of doing so in this case is that the same institutions may be supply elements at one time and in one circumstance but demand elements at other times and under differing circumstances. For example, business corporations are important elements in these markets and usually on the borrowing side of both the money and capital markets. Nevertheless, most large corporations are also important lenders in the money markets.

REVISION

As with other markets, breaking down financial markets into supply and demand makes analysis easier. But the same institutions may be supply elements at one time and circumstance and demand elements at another. Corporations, for example, usually borrowers in both money and capital markets, are also important lenders in the money markets. (LF 47%)

Much of the awkwardness we've been chronicling comes from an exaggerated desire for precision. The authors spell everything out. People writing government regulations are specially fond of this habit. If we number every streak of the tulip, somehow that will make instantly clear what the tulip is like, focus essence through an enumeration of particulars. So in the following piece of Official Style:

MOTOR VEHICLE SAFETY STANDARD NO. 217
Bus Window Retention and Release
(Docket No. 2–10; Notice 3)
The standard requires emergency exit location markings to be placed in certain occupant spaces because of a possible contradiction under the proposed standard between the requirement that the identification markings be located

27

within 6 inches of the point of operation and the requirement that the markings be visible to a seated occupant. The NHTSA has concluded that emergency egress could be hindered if the passenger has difficulty in finding the marking, and that location of the marking outside of an occupant space containing an adjacent seat, which could be permitted under the proposed standard, could create this problem. At the same time it is desirable for the identification and instructions to be located near the point of release. Therefore the final rule requires that when a release mechanism is not located within an occupant space containing an adjacent seat, a label indicating the location of the nearest release mechanism shall be placed within the occupant space.

Business people must cope with this kind of prose every day. The usual Official Style problems present themselves—the "is" + prepositional phrase habit, the shopping bag shape, and especially a wonderful bureaucratic fondness for spelling out the obvious, as in "emergency egress could be hindered if the passenger has difficulty in finding the marking."

But above all it lacks *focus*. We don't know which assertions are central, which are derivative and subordinate. Again, a problem of who's kicking who, but this time on a paragraph as well as a sentence level. Let's try the Paramedic Method here, only this time adding two more diagnostic procedures:

1. Circle the prepositions.
2. Circle the "is" forms.
3. Ask "Who is kicking who?"
4. Put this "kicking" action in a simple (not compound) active verb.
5. Start fast—no mindless introductions.
6. Write out each sentence on a blank sheet of paper and mark off its basic rhythmic units with a "/".
7. Read the passage aloud with emphasis and feeling.

28

I'm not sure, though, what the passage means. No cheap shot intended; writing this kind of detailed instruction is hard. If I've mistaken the meaning in my revision, try one of your own.

Here goes. We are in a bus, trying to decide where to put the emergency exit signs that indicate a pop-out window. Standard No. 217 requires that in addition to the emergency exit signs placed next to the pop-out windows themselves, signs pointing to the exits be placed in rows of seats not next to pop-out windows. Thus everyone not sitting next to an exit window will be directed to one. A good deal of specific detail accompanies this central rule. What we need, then, is a short and emphatic opening sentence that will tell us what we're doing. Notice how badly the opening sentence does this job. Here it is again:

> The standard requires emergency exit location markings to be placed in certain occupant spaces because of a possible contradiction under the proposed standard between the requirement that the identification markings be located within 6 inches of the point of operation and the require-ment that the markings be visible to a seated occupant.

Too many things are happening on the same level:

1. Emergency exit location markings have to be placed in "certain occupant spaces," but those spaces are not defined until later.
2. A possible contradiction exists between the two other requirements.
3. Signs 6″ from the window.
4. Signs to be visible to a seated occupant.

Two ways to skin this cat. Either you can start with a causal sequence: The proposed standard requires both (3) and (4) and they conflict. *Therefore* we propose the following. Or you can start with the new standard itself and then explain how it came to be. Let's try both openings and see which is better.

29

REVISION 1

The proposed standard requires two things: (1) emergency window exit signs must be within 6″ of the window; (2) every seated passenger must be able to see the sign. These two requirements sometimes conflict. If you are sitting in a row of seats not next to an emergency window, you won't be able to see the sign. Standard 217 requires that these rows have a sign directing you to the emergency window.

Or

REVISION 2

Standard 217 requires that seat rows not next to emergency exit windows include signs directing passengers to the exit windows. The present standard includes two provisions that conflict. First, every emergency window exit must be marked by a sign within 6″ of the window. Second, every seated passenger must be able to see the sign. But what about passengers seated in rows not next to an emergency window? They might not be able to see the sign. NHTSA has concluded that signs should be placed in those rows directing passengers to the emergency windows.

These revisions take care of the first paragraph. Word-counts for the sentences run this way:

- Original: 52–46–20–38
- Revision 1: 30–5–23–15
- Revision 2: 20–8–16–11–13–9–17

The revisions vary the sentence length more but, more important, they make them all shorter. A very long sentence, to stay in your head all at once, has to have a very clear framework. It may use parallelism, parenthesis, contrasts, alliteration, a whole repertoire of patterns. Without these patterns as a guide, the reader soon gets lost. Shorter sentences solve the problem in a different way. In the revisions, the central idea—because two requirements conflict, we need a third—occurs in two different ways but takes a spotlight in both. Which revision is better? The first, probably. Shorter than the second (71 words against 94; LF 54% and 39%), it also uses the short/long focusing strategy better.

The PM revisions have done other things besides vary sentence length, to be sure. The "is" + preposition formula has been broken up, the diction simplified ("location marking" = "sign"), the reader has been reassigned his humanity ("you" for "occupant"), and the sentences given a little shape. As a result of these changes, the passage's central assertion seems a little clearer. Maybe we could revise yet again.

REVISION 3

The proposed Standard 217 requires three things: (1) emergency window exit signs must be within 6″ of the window; (2) seated passengers must be able to see the signs; (3) if they can't see the window signs, post an extra sign they can see.

Radical therapy, this. We've left out the "possible contradiction" thread of the argument. But look what has been gained: LF 75%; paragraph reduced to one sentence; above all, *focus*. The regulation's essence leaps to the eye. Sentence shape supplies exactly the kind of specificity needed. Each revision represents a trade-off between emphasis and detail. Wouldn't the third be the best bet if you were writing Standard 217?

Shaping a sentence, then, means focusing an idea. Look at the following shapeless blur:

We are not anxious to casually spend the company's money but our recommendation is intended to minimize the risk involved in launching a new product and a new category into an environment where there exists a vacuum of current knowledge and interest from both consumer and retailer.

31

Here the chick struggling out of the egg depends on contrast: a *bad* way to spend the company's money (needless research) versus a *good* way to spend the company's money (research that launches a product with minimum risk). The sentence as written smears this contrast over five lines. Neither eye nor ear gives the mind any help. How do we get these two powerful allies on our side? How about this:

> We don't want to waste the company's money on needless research, but informative research can save money in launching a new product, especially in an unknown market.

We've set up an "X" pattern that brings the contrast to quick visual focus.

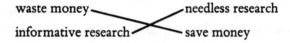

You put contrasted ideas in similar phrases ("waste money" and "save money"; "needless research" and "informative research"). You invert the basic order in the second element— "money . . . research" becomes "research . . . money" to show that you have inverted the cash flow. And the new visual shape invites the voice to point up the contrast; stress "waste" and "needless" in the first element, "informative" and "save" in the second. A little final guff-removal converts "into an environment where there exists a vacuum of current knowledge and interest from both consumer and retailer" into "especially in an unknown market."

Here are the original and the revision again:

ORIGINAL

We are not anxious to casually spend the company's money but our recommendation is intended to minimize the risk involved in launching a new product and a new category into an environment where there exists a vacuum of current knowledge and interest from both consumer and retailer. (47 words)

REVISION

We don't want to waste the company's money on needless research, but informative research can save money in launching a new product, especially in an unknown market. (27 words)

A sentence whose shape helps launch its idea and a lard factor fo 43%—a sentence half as long and twice as good. And think of the back pressure: writing prose that *sees* clearly may help us to *think* clearly.

Here is another little shopping baglet. But now the blurring comes less from ineptitude than from design:

> As indicated previously, it would be speculative to attempt a prediction of the financial liability of the public airport proprietor in the event it had to bear the financial responsibility for damage under judgments made against it on account of aircraft noise.

Financial liability poses a sticky wicket for this writer of an Environmental Impact Statement. The City Fathers who want to buy the airport hired him to write the report, and they don't want this appalling liability spectre to make the scene. If the writer had been an ordinary citizen and not a hired gun, he or she might have just said, "Nobody has any idea how much money aircraft noise suits could cost the city." But that skillful side-by-side placement of the two parallel central elements—"has any idea" and "how much money"—detonated just the land-mine that the writer has been tiptoeing around. Notice how the eye leads the voice to wrap itself around "has any idea," to raise both pinch and stress when you pronounce it? To avoid this, the writer has taken refuge in the full Official Style. Look again:

33

As indicated previously, it would be speculative to attempt a prediction of the financial liability of the public airport proprietor in the event it had to bear the financial responsibility for damage under judgments made against it on account of aircraft noise.

The standard Official Style drill:

1. "To be" verb (here "would be") plus a string of prepositional phrases.
2. Kicker evaporated out of sight in an impersonal construction ("it would be speculative").
3. Real verb *predict* stuffed safely out of sight down in "to attempt a prediction of."
4. Really scary verb *(pay)* really stuffed out of sight in "bear the financial liability for."

The Official Style smears the point out into a 42-word bag. Our common sense version—"Nobody has any idea how much money aircraft-noise suits could cost the city"—focuses the point in 14 (LF 66%).

As a last example of prose shapelessness, look at this letter from a cosmetics company to a design firm:

Pheramone Fragrances, Inc. is evaluating its corporate design needs for the near and intermediate term. The purpose of this effort is to determine how the image of the company might be best promoted or modified to assist us in meeting our growth goals. Your firm is one of the eight firms who have either been in contact with us or who have been recommended by our senior advisors as having the requisite talent, skills, and experience to assist us in this effort. Our plan is to conduct a detailed review of all submissions and to select three or four firms to meet with our executive staff and senior advisors to present any additional materials or information they desire. The design services the company employs must be able to make a positive contribution toward this goal in terms of the external image, awareness, and recognition of Pheramone as a leader in its field.

Not bad prose—just boring, lifeless. You notice first the bad match between a cosmetics company, which must be sensitive to style above all, and the stylistic *insensitivity* of a prose like this. If their corporate image—and their products—are as lumpen as this, no wonder they need some design help. The way a company writes *is* a logo, the most revealing one of all. Prose style always carries this symbolic charge, declares how sensitive, or insensitive, a company is to the whole stylistic dimension of human behavior. Here, a diastrous mismatch.

Notice, for a start, how four of the five sentences use the same verb, "is"—the weakest, most listless, least specific propellant a sentence can use:

> Pheramone Fragrances, Inc. *is* evaluating . . .
> The purpose of this effort *is* to determine . . .
> Your firm *is* one . . .
> Our plan *is* to conduct . . .

Prose like this declares: "We have no imagination! We cannot see language! We cannot hear it! We are not easily bored! We love formulaic thinking! Above all, we like slow openings, take our time getting to the point, and like to say everything at least twice." A cosmetics company ought not to write this way, but more important they ought not to *think* this way. No wonder they have an image problem.

Again, so easy to fix. Let's start with the first two sentences:

ORIGINAL

Pheramone Fragrances, Inc. is evaluating its corporate design needs for the near and intermediate term. The purpose of this effort is to determine how the image of the company might be best promoted or modified to assist us in meeting our growth goals.

You are struck first, in these two sentences, by what we might call an *action blur*. All kinds of actions are suggested but none are stressed or focused. "Evaluating," "design," "needs," "purpose," "effort," "determine," "image," "promoted," "modified," "assist," "meeting," "growth." A dozen possible actions are first suggested and then smeared across the sentence. Again, the symbolism grabs you by the lapel: here is a company that does not know what to do first or at all. The sentence models, in the most graphic way possible, a management failure—a failure to think. Instead of thought, it gives us the history—through all those nascent actions—of its attempts to think. This constitutes the business equivalent of the student's paper about how hard it is to write a paper. What action should stand center stage? *Need*. "Pheramone Fragrances, Inc. needs . . ." All right. What does it need? To change its image. Why? To increase sales. This sequence stands at the center of the assertion:

REVISION

Pheramone Fragrances, Inc. needs to improve its image in order to increase sales.

Why not just say this? Because it *does not sound impressive enough*. And so we add needless specificity—"near and intermediate term." You use two words "promoted or modified," where one will do. You string prepositional phrases together with infinitives into our standard laundry list. This makes the prose not only shapeless but pompous.

The rest is easy:

Your firm is one of eight from whom we have requested submissions. We will review the submissions and ask three or four firms to meet with our senior staff. The design service finally selected must show Pheramone how to present itself as a leader in its field.

And do we really need the last sentence at all? Doesn't it go without saying? Why else would they hire a design firm?

I need to beat this dead cosmetics horse one more time to make an important point. Look again at the last sentence:

The design services the company employs must be able to make a positive contribution toward this goal in terms of the external image, awareness, and recognition of Pheramone as a leader in its field.

Action! Action! Action! *Contribute,* not "be able to make a positive contribution toward." See how this circumlocution smears the action across eight words when you need only one? And what does "in terms of" really mean? How does it relate to "external image"? And what other kinds of image besides "external" can be meant here anyway? And who is aware of what in "awareness"? Who is recognizing whom? The worst mistake a business person can make is to lose track of who is doing what to whom. Who is kicking who? Here all the actions are so vague and smeared you don't know what is going on or who is where. This muddled action is not a trifling matter. It points directly to the muddled thought that makes Pheramone spend a lot of money to park up its image.

Here is the original again. Read it aloud and without hurry:

ORIGINAL

Pheramone Fragrances, Inc. is evaluating its corporate design needs for the near and intermediate term. The purpose of this effort is to determine how the image of the company might be best promoted or modified to assist us in meeting our growth goals. Your firm is one of the eight firms who have either been in contact with us or who have been recommended by our senior advisors as having the requisite talent, skills, and experience to assist us in this effort. Our plan is to conduct a detailed review of all submissions and to select three or four firms to meet with our executive staff and senior advisors to present any additional materials or information they desire. The design services the company employs must be able to make a

37

positive contribution toward this goal in terms of the external image, awareness, and recognition of Pheramone as a leader in its field.

Here is the revision:

REVISION

Pheramone Fragrances, Inc. needs to improve its corporate image to increase sales. Your firm is one of eight from whom we have received design proposals. We will review the proposals and ask three or four firms to meet with our senior staff before we make a final choice.

Business folk like to think themselves blunt bottom-liners to a person, but they very seldom write that way. If this plain opening seems too blunt or bald, ask yourself why. Is it the kind of need a company should be embarrassed about? Or pompous about, to cover over the embarrassment? We have cut the passage by two thirds (50 words instead of 151). Gone the blurred action, the pomposity, the sheer mindless guff. Have we sacrificed a ceremonial courtesy, or a euphemistic delicacy about final purpose, in doing so? I think not, but it is interesting to argue the other side. Try an alternative revision with it in mind.

CHAPTER 3

Voicing, Sentence Length, Rhythm, and Sound

Take a piece of your prose and a red pencil and draw a slash after every sentence. Two or three pages ought to make a large enough sample. If the red marks occur at regular intervals, you have, as they used to say in the White House, a problem. You can chart the problem another way, if you like. Choose a standard length for one sentence and then do a bar graph. If it looks like this,

---

---

dandy. If like this,

---

not so dandy. Obviously, no absolute quantitative standards exist for how much variety is good, how little bad, but the principle couldn't be easier. Vary sentence length. Naturally enough, complex patterns will fall into long sentences, and emphatic conclusions work well when short. But no general rule prevails except to avoid monotony. When you think about sentence length in a *particular* case, of course, all the other concomitant variables of style enter in since they determine sentence length to begin with. You can't revise a passage *only* to vary sentence length. In fact, a varied pattern usually reflects other stylistic choices already made, rather than being an end in itself; it represents a relative virtue not an absolute one, an appearance of health rather than a vital sign. But it does provide an easy place to begin *voicing* your prose, giving it a recognizable and forceful human personality.

We can now add one last rule to the PM:

1. Circle the prepositions.
2. Circle the "is" forms.
3. Ask "Who is kicking who?"
4. Put this "kicking" action in a simple (not compound) active verb.
5. Start fast—no mindless introductions.
6. Write out each sentence on a blank sheet of paper and mark off its basic rhythmic units with a "/".
7. Read the passage aloud with emphasis and feeling.
8. Mark off sentence lengths in the passage with a "/".

Let's try rule 8 of the following passage:

ORIGINAL

It is important to bring forth the problems and other obstacles that are hindering our performance and growth. / To be successful we must grow and to grow we must identify our problems and deal with them. / Time will be allowed for discussions after each presentation to focus on the problems and potential solutions. /

40

Not too promising. How does the bar graph look?

_____ (18 words)
_____ (18)
_____ (17)

Again, this kind of external measurement does not provide an infallible rule. It offers only a way into sentence voicing, an external trigger to internal problems. Here, there is no voice, only a bland impersonality. We'll see what happens to voice when we try to break up that monotonous sentence length problem:

ORIGINAL

It is important to bring forth the problems and other obstacles that are hindering our performance and growth.

REVISION

What problems hinder our performance and growth?

No more dead-rocket opening ("It is important to bring forth . . ."). A 61% lard factor. No more needless repetition ("problems and other obstacles"). A seven-word sentence to break up the 18–18–17 pattern. But above all a definite and direct voice.

With a seven-word sentence preceding, we can leave the second one pretty much as is:

ORIGINAL

To be successful we must grow and to grow we must identify our problems and deal with them.

REVISION

To succeed we must grow and to grow we must identify our problems and deal with them.

We need only change "to be" plus an adjective ("to be successful") to the simple and much stronger infinitive "to

41

succeed"). Notice how this change strengthens the natural power of the AB:BC pattern of "To succeed—grow: to grow—identify"? The voice in this sentence comes across clearly; furthermore, it gains power from the clear voicing of the previous sentence. Thus is a prose personality born.

ORIGINAL

Time will be allowed for discussions after each presentation to focus on the problems and potential solutions.

REVISION

After each presentation, we will discuss problems and possible solutions.

We have followed rule 3 of the PM, found the actor ("we"), and given ourselves (rule 4) a simple active verb ("discuss"). We have followed rule 5, too; we have started faster and gotten much sooner to the "discuss problems" heart of the sentence. If we follow rule 7, read the sentence aloud with emphasis and feeling, it sounds pretty good. Try it. The "triple p" pattern of "*p*resentation," "*p*roblems," and "*p*ossible" adds an alliterative smoothness that doesn't obtrude. Sound works with sense.

Now the original again and the revision:

ORIGINAL

It is important to bring forth the problems and other obstacles that are hindering our performance and growth. / To be successful we must grow and to grow we must identify our problems and deal with them. / Time will be allowed for discussions after each presentation to focus on the problems and potential solutions. /

REVISION

What problems hinder our performance and growth? / To succeed we must grow and to grow we must identify these problems and deal with them. / After each presentation, we will discuss both problems and possible solutions. /

I've tinkered a little further with the revision here. You almost always have to revise for continuity when you reunite sentences revised separately. The bar graph now looks like this:

——————— (7)
——————————————— (17)
————————— (11)

We have a more varied pattern, and the voice and emphasis that usually comes with it.

If we can hazard one generalization about sentence length in business writing, it must be this: sentences are almost always too long. A general spirit of dieselizing pervades the office; the engine wants to run on long after you have turned off the key of content. Usually it is a snap to fix.

ORIGINAL

In developing software, we had to begin from scratch; that is, we were unable to build on previously developed programs.

REVISION

In developing software, we had to begin from scratch.

Again, half as long, twice as strong.

When the sentences all go on too long, prose seems a swamp to the reader. Look at the following typical example:

Another characteristic of the traditional life cycle is that there is a clear single-string path identified to the user and to DP from the original feasibility study out through to the implementation of the system. / Finally, a characteristic that renders the system development life cycle unpopular with programmers is the fact that it forces heavy documentation at all stages. / Therefore, some of the perceived disadvantages of systems development life cycle methods are that they can be cumbersome and are sometimes thought to slow down the project. / Additionally, techni-

43

cians may complain that such rigidity is stifling their creativity. / Finally, the result of the use of all these new techniques and methods is that the user and DP functions are becoming merged and the DP development group is being regarded as a service area to the user and in many organizations is being made part of the user group. / The important fundamental to remember is that, even with this apparently dramatic reduction in the length of the system's development life cycle, the basic needs of the original seven stages must still be met, however "hidden" these stages may be. /

The bar graph looks like this:

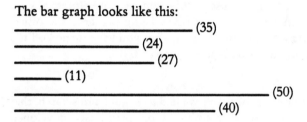

But the variety here is lost because almost all the sentences go on so long. You crave a quick three- or four-word exclamation. Something with a little zip and emphasis. Try putting the PM to work here yourself; that relatively short 11-word sentence in the middle looks like a promising place to begin.

The credit manager who wrote the following memo avoids all the dangers of the prose swamp we have just waded through:

What can the sales force do to help?

1. *Anticipate* problems with your accounts. If a credit memo needs to be issued before an invoice can be paid, be sure the proper steps leading to the issuance of the credit memo are taken. Look for and help us remove other "roadblocks" to payment—wrong P.O. numbers, etc.

2. Talk to your customers. Let them know that we appreciate their business and the *prompt payment* of our invoices. Point out the advantages of a good track record with us.

3. Pounce on your past dues early in the month. Go over those statement sheets we give you. Assist where and how you can. Balances cleared by the 10th will insure no interruptions of service, untimely "holds," etc.

4. Keep the credit department informed. Fill us in, and help us to keep the flow of money and orders going.

What a terrific memo! Not a word wasted. A direct voice that emerges from a vivid series of imperatives: "Anticipate . . . Talk to . . . Let them know . . . Point out . . . Pounce on . . . Go over . . . Keep . . . Fill us in." This is a natural consequence from the basic strategy: an opening imperative, then detailed instructions following. Sentence length and rhythm create a clear prose personality, friendly and cordial but energetic and in control, and expecting you to be as well. You know just where you are, who is kicking who. Every sentence starts fast. The life, and the frustrations, of commerce lurk in every line.

The elements of prose style—grammar, syntax, shape, rhythm, emphasis, level of usage, and so on—all work as dependent variables. Change one and you change the rest. But of them all, rhythm constitutes the most vital of prose's vital life-signs. Rhythmless, unemphatic prose always indicates that something has gone wrong. And Tin Ears, insensitivity to the sounds of words, indicate that the hearing that registers rhythm has been turned off.

Tin Ears have become so common that often you can't tell mistakes from intentions. Here is an advertising flack for the Army, engaged in that traditional business activity—recruitment:

Like any new departure in motivating men, the path to a Modern Volunteer Army is beset with perils and pitfalls but it also has potential for progress.

Is the alliteration of "*m*otivating *m*en," "*p*erils and *p*itfalls," "*p*otential for *p*rogress" intended or accidental? It works, at all events, obvious though it may be. The three central phrases of the sentence are spotlighted by an alliterated pair of words, and the last two pairs are put into almost visual contrast:

perils and pitfalls
potential for progress

And "motivating men" finds an alliterative echo in "Modern" while the *p* alliteration has a pre-echo in "path." All this seems to indicate premeditation and a heavy hand. But the writer obviously creates a specific shape and rhythm.

Let's turn the tables for a minute. We'll give the tired business writer a break and take an example from her critic, the writer who writes about writing:

For the writer, the practice of bad writing is harmful, for it results in an inhibition of his responses to intellectual and imaginative stimuli.

Notice the "*in an in*hibition" sequence, forcing the reader to babble? And did the writer see the "harm*ful for*" doublet? Notice how it works against his purpose here? The punctuation encourages us to stop after "harmful" while the *ful–for* alliterative couplet wants us to rush on without a stop. And he has another mouthful-of-peanut-butter *'n–m* cluster in "re-sponses to *in*tellectual and *im*aginative sti*m*uli." I've deliberately chosen an example where this unspeakable cluster did *not* stand out, just to show how often one is there, nevertheless. Prose will always possess a spoken dimension so long as we continue to speak. If we ignore it, it will not go away; it will come back to plague us. How to fix this example? First, the standard drill. Circle the prepositions. Get rid of "is." Ask who is kicking who. Squeeze out the lard. Here is the original again:

For the writer, the practice of bad writing is harmful, for it results in an inhibition of his responses to intellectual and imaginative stimuli.

The actor is "bad writing" and the action lies buried in "inhibition." So: "Bad writing inhibits a writer's intellect and imagination" (LF 66%). "The practice of" is one of those "the fact that" fillers. "Results in an inhibition of" is one of those "is" + noun + preposition substitutions for the simple verb "inhibits," like "stands in violation of" for "violates." "Harmful" is implied by "inhibits." "Responses to intellectual and imaginative stimuli," means simply "intellect and imagination." And so we have "Bad writing inhibits a writer's intellect and imagination." And, since our subject is Tin Ears, we notice right away that "mind" instead of "intellect" smooths out that *intellect* and *imagination* cluster of *m*'s, *n*'s, and *t*'s. "Bad writing inhibits a writer's mind and imagination." We've also substituted a single-syllable word for a three-syllable word, and this helps out in a sentence already overloaded with two- and three-syllable words. Notice how they monotonize the rhythm?

What has happened here? We've revised the sentence with our do-it-yourself PM and the rhythmless morass has taken care of itself. Interdependent variables, again. Find out who is kicking who, and the problems that fan out from this central misapprehension may solve themselves. Let's mark the original sentence for rhythm. I'll put a slash for each cadence:

> For the writer / the practice / of bad writing / is harmful / for it results / in an inhibition / of his responses / to intellectual / and imaginative / stimuli.

Every unit runs to almost the same length—da-da-dum, da-da-dum. You can see how the prepositional phrases, strung out like a snake's vertebrae, prohibit any life or vigor. The revision, while not "Shall I compare thee to a summer's day," at least has components of different sizes:

> Bad writing / inhibits a writer's mind / and imagination.

The stress falls naturally at the end, where we want it, on "mind" and "imagination." (What would happen to this concluding stress if we said "mind and heart" instead? Would it make the concluding rhythmic unit better or worse?)

Squeezing the lard out of prose seems sometimes to liberate a natural rhythm, modest but clear, that was waiting to be freed. Look at this before-and-after nugget of business reporting:

BEFORE

Whereas the President emerges more as a victor, the Chairman seems defeated.

AFTER

The President seems to win, the Chairman to lose.

A lard factor of 25% obscures the natural modest stress on "wins" and "loses." Often rhythmic emphasis, once we are sensitive to it, will tell us what to pare away.

So, too, will the level of formality we strive for. Business people, in their everyday worklife, don't usually wear stuffed shirts. An easy first-name informality seems far more common. Yet when someone starts to write, what comes out often sounds more like a royal proclamation than a simple exchange of information. Americans have always had trouble with public formality of any sort, from dress to architecture. Maybe that fuels our fondness for the formulas of the Official Style; once we learn them, we can just pour our information into them and forget it. But whatever the reason, colloquial directness occurs rarely in business writing. When a sales manager introduces his colleagues to a new product with "Our baby needs a new name," he illustrates informality at its most efficient—and rarest. So too the sales rep who begins his monthly report with "*Wow!* What a month!" And this expression of not entirely good-humored vexation projects the same conversational power:

Well, Jack, another C-303 Program Review has come and gone without advising ABC Control. Contrary to popular

belief, we are interested in supporting program management, but we can't do it if we are not part of the team.

This memo needs nothing but praise. The writer seeks to
convey not only a fact—once again his office has not been
consulted about a review—but his attitude toward that failure
and how it affects company welfare. A polite expression of
legitimate vexation and anger sometimes works wonders.
When you try to do it in the Official Style, though, you often
sound stilted and silly:

Dear Roy:

The purpose of this letter is to make you formally aware
of a maintenance situation that has become grossly intoler-
able and thus requires immediate remedial action by Derivative Digital Devices (DDD). Since April 2, 1984, DDD
field maintenance personnel and Quirky Printer personnel
have attempted to fix our system printer, model number
oh, oh, oh, oh. (Attached is a list of available service record
receipt numbers.) We are rapidly approaching the four-
month mark and our printer is still performing below
reasonable acceptable standards. What is probably untypical is the amount of patience and cooperation I've shown in
waiting for DDD field maintenance to resolve this problem. I can no longer wait and therefore urgently request
that you motivate at DDD whatever level of authority is
required to correct this situation immediately in a manner
that is fully acceptable to Anodyne Corp.
Should this letter prove ineffectual in obtaining results, I
shall assume that you have abdicated your responsibilities
and that I am left to my own resources in dealing with
DDD management.

You can see why the writer fell into this style; he wanted the
minatory force of a legalistic-sounding warning. But the
subject just cries out for the opposite strategy, for a "Look,

Jack, if you don't fix this bleeping printer, I'm going to come on over to DDD and start knocking on doors and when I'm finished you'll wish you'd never been born." At the least, the writer ought to have drawn closer to a conversational tone. *Not:* "What is probably untypical is the amount of patience and cooperation I've shown in waiting for DDD field maintenance to resolve this problem." *Instead:* "I've shown the patience of Job in waiting for your people to fix this problem." *Not:* "I can no longer wait and therefore urgently request that you motivate at DDD whatever level of authority is required to correct this situation immediately in a manner that is fully acceptable to Anodyne Corp." *Instead:* "I can't wait any longer. Find somebody—I don't care at what level—who can fix this printer." Impatience at incompetence is often justifiable in the business world. It can be expressed through a cold and detached legalistic prose, but usually conversational directness works much better.

Compare the voice, the sense of human personality, behind the written utterance, in the two following passages about pay and promotion.

Review of the Compensation Structure for Engineers reveals we are appropriately competitive to retain present good Engineers and to successfully attract new talent from the labor market. The weakest point in our wage structure is to competitively compensate new Engineers after they are two or three years into their experience spectrum. This problem results from the need to give these Engineers merit increases that better the annual inflation rate to keep them ahead of the starting salaries of new college graduates.

How do we stimulate and reward high performance when promotions will be scarce and competition for them fierce?

The first passage cries out for the PM treatment. Circle the prepositions and infinitives (split or whole) and the "is" forms. Try to find the action. Do a bar graph of sentence length and then try to give the sentences some kind of shape and rhythm related to the human voice.

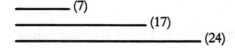

Too much of a length and too long. How about something like:

REVISION

We pay our engineers competitive beginning salaries. After a couple of years, though, their salaries tend to fall behind those of new college graduates. How do we give them merit increases that stay ahead both of inflation and the beginning salaries of people who have been hired later?

The bar graph looks a little better in the revision:

————— (7)
——————————— (17)
————————————— (24)

My revision may not be a world-beater (too many "of" phrases for a start, including two in a row), but at least it breaks up the monotony of the passage and moves it several steps toward the crisp conversational voice that makes the second passage good prose.

Prose rhythm, then, does not simply paint a gloss over meaning but helps constitute it. Often the rhythm will say as much as the "meaning." So in this brief example:

The month of April has been spent, for the most part, in assessment of problems and possible solutions, settling priorities, and building and orienting the Task Force. Therefore, most of the accomplishments, although real, are intangible.

The hesitant, broken, back-and-forth rhythm projects a disastrous impression of indecisive muddle. "Well, uh, er, we have had only a, uh, month to try to, you know, get the whole Task Force going and even so we've managed, like, to get quite a lot done, really, I mean considering the time we've had." Who knows, they really may have done a terrific job, however "intangible." *But the prose makes it sound just the opposite.* It says one thing in matter, another in manner.

Sometimes, too, a sentence rhythm will seem worth aiming at just for the sound of it, for the music. Look at how a long string of one-syllable words breaks up the rhythm here:

The Director's overwhelming presence in relation *to that of the rest of the* employees strikes us immediately.

Seven one-syllable words in a row dulls the prose bite as well as a string of jawbreakers does. Again, the villain is that string of prepositional phrases. The fix simply lines up kicker and kickee:

The Director, obviously, overwhelms the other employees.

(Do you see the similarity, *within* the sentence, to the problem of varying length from sentence to sentence?) Once your ears have had their consciousness raised, they'll catch the easy sound problems as they flow from the pen—"however clever" will become "however shrewd" in the first draft—and the harder ones will seem easier to revise.

Let's try one last revision, massage a passage that shows just how the Official Style works against a voiced prose, against any rhythm and shape and thus personality in the sentence. I'll put this whole definition of a Program Manager before you, and then we'll dissect it:

With regard to your request concerning Program Management and specifically the definition and function of a Program Manager, the following is submitted:

A Program Manager reports to the General Manager and is a member of his staff.

A Program Manager's authority is that of a Director but may be authorized with more authority as designated by the General Manager.

The specific assignment of a Program Manager is to administer a program in its entirety.

The planning function of the program is a responsibility of the Program Manager.

Coordination with the Operating Departments is a necessary activity that the Program Manager must maintain. This coordination effort requires that the functional areas involved be kept aware of what is being enforced so as not to allow this condition to become habitual.

The Program Manager may develop alternative methods of achieving the program goals within accepted organizational parameters. This option is based on the personality of the Program Manager and the nature of the program. This option is limited to the organizational procedures and should not drift far from the norm but should allow for flexibility.

Wallboard prose. The same homogeneous Official Style from beginning to end, cut up by a circular saw into arbitrary sentences. The sentences are assembled strictly according to the Official Style formula of "is" plus prepositional phrase strings:

A Program Manager's authority
    is that
    of a Director but may be authorized
    with more authority
    as designated
    by the General Manager.

The planning function
of the program
is a responsibility
of the Program Manager.

This option
is based
on the personality
of the Program Manager and the nature
of the program.

The actor is hidden in a god-like impersonal construction: "the following is submitted." The sentences use the slow wind-up, "The blah-blah of the blah-blah is that," opening formula. And what about sentence length?

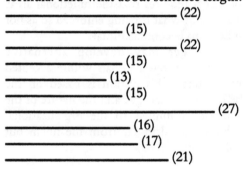

Not much variation and all long; standard wallboard sizes. If you try rule 6 of the PM—marking out rhythmic lengths—you get something like this.

The specific assignment / of a Program Manager / is to administer / a program / in its entirety.

This option / is based / on the personality / of the Program Manager / and the nature / of the program.

The phrases too come in standard wallboard sizes; tedium itself. But it is when you try applying rule 7 of the PM—reading the passage aloud with feeling and emphasis—that the pompous emptiness of its tautological pronouncements really comes across. Try it. Makes you giggle, doesn't it?

We can see, in a passage like this, how all the variables of the Official Style interlock. The lifeless, verbless impersonality leads to the "is" plus prepositional phrase strings which, in turn, lead to the monotonous sentence lengths and phrase lengths, which, in their turn, prohibit any sentence rhythm, and this leads in its turn to voiceless prose, dehumanized and dead. All these attributes constitute, of course, everything that good business prose ought not to be. When we try to revise a passage like this, it literally comes apart in our hands, falls into its constituent pieces and reveals the striking vacuity of its thought. We'll need a sentence-by-sentence revision to see this:

ORIGINAL

With regard to your request concerning Program Management and specifically the definition and function of a Program Manager, the following is submitted:

REVISION

You ask for a job description of Program Manager:

ORIGINAL

A Program Manager reports to the General Manager and is a member of his staff.

REVISION

A Program Manager reports to the General Manager and is on his staff.

ORIGINAL

A Program Manager's authority is that of a Director but may be authorized with more authority as designated by the General Manager.

55

REVISION

A Program Manager ranks as a Director, but may be given more authority by the General Manager. [I am trying to escape the "authority . . . authorized with more authority" tautological repetition here.]

ORIGINAL

The specific assignment of a Program Manager is to administer a program in its entirety. The planning function of the program is a responsibility of the Program Manager.

REVISION

A Program Manager plans and administers a program.

Maybe we don't need to do the whole thing after all. The last revision, with its lard factor of 75%, shows the central vice of the whole passage—empty tautology, a definition that repeats the same word (e.g., "authority") without defining it. The thinking becomes so general and vague that finally the writer starts using words (e.g., "this condition" in the penultimate paragraph) that refer to nothing at all.

Job descriptions are written for people and ought to sound that way. When you have finished applying the PM to a passage like this, a voice with at least some relation to humankind ought to emerge of its own accord. Let me try a last, slightly impressionistic, revision:

REVISION

You ask me to define a Program Manager. A Program Manager plans and administers a program and coordinates it with other departments. Reporting to the General Manager and on his staff, a Program Manager ranks as a Director but may be given additional authority by the General Manager.

I've rearranged things a little and left out over half the original. What I've omitted seems to me pure guff. Do you agree? Even if I have left out some details, the recognizable human voice that enters justifies the omission. In the large organizations that need specific job descriptions like this, details fall as thick as snowflakes in Siberia. The recognizable human voice that will state the pattern beyond the detail and act on it lies much thinner on the ground. It's that recognizable and responsible voice we should aim for.

CHAPTER 4

The Official Style

Up to now we've been analyzing particular stylistic elements—shape, rhythm, emphasis. We've seen, in the process, that these elements are interrelated, that they seem to proceed from the same aesthetic, that they constitute a common style. In the examples we've been revising, we've been in effect translating from the Official Style into plain English. Now we are going to do this directly, focus on the Official Style as an exercise in stylistic analysis and translation. At the same time, we'll try, instead of simply condemning the Official Style, to ask how and why it has come about, how it works in the world.

Students of style have traditionally distinguished three basic levels—high, middle, low. The content of these categories varied somewhat, but usually the high style was a formal and ornamental style for a solemn and ritualized occasion, the low style enshrined the loose and sloppy intercourse of daily life, and the middle style stood somewhere in between. Since World War II, American prose has worked a pronounced variation on this enduring pattern. The low style has pretty much disintegrated into a series of "I-mean-like-you-know" shrugs and spastic tics, like, you know? And as we have come to suspect fancy language and formal ceremony as undemocratic, we have come to suspect the high style, too. As a substitute, we've clasped to our bosoms the Official Style—a style that is formal without ever pretending to be grand. The Official Style is often stigmatized as bureaucratese or jargon

59

and often is both. But it is a genuine style, and one that reflects the genuine bureaucratization of American life. It has its own rules and its own ambitions, and anyone writing in business or government nowadays in America must come to know both. The Official Style comes to us in two main guises, as the language of social science and as the language of bureaucracy. Social science wants above all to sound scientific—disinterested, impersonal, factual. Bureaucracy wants above all to sound official—neutral, formal, authoritative, inevitable. Both ambitions converge on a common set of verbal habits, the Official Style.

The Official Style runs from school days to retirement. As soon as you realize that you live "in a system," whether P.S. 41, the University of California, the Department of Agriculture, or General Motors, you start developing the Official Style. Used unthinkingly, it provides the quickest tip-off that you have become system-sick and look at life only through the system's eyes. It is a scribal style, ritualized, formulaic, using a special vocabulary to describe a special kind of world, the world of bureaucratic officialdom. And it is, increasingly, the only kind of prose style America ever sees. It is also, along with the social changes that sponsor it, the main reason for our prose problem. The low style has dissolved, the high style has hardened and dehydrated, and the middle style has simply evaporated. The Official Style threatens to replace all three.

If you can analyze, write, and translate it, maybe you can find your niche in the System—public sector or private—without losing your soul to it. For you may have to write in the Official Style, but you don't have to think in it. If you are the first on the scene after the sports car has missed the curve, climbed the hedge, and ended up on the lawn, you won't ask the driver, as did one policeman, "How, uh, sir, did you achieve this configuration?"

Sometimes you can see the Official Style seizing its prey like a boa constrictor and gradually squeezing the life out of it. Here's a college student first feeling its grip.

Twelve-year-old boys like to fight. Consequently, on several occasions I explained to them the negative aspects of fighting. Other responsibilities included keeping them dry (when near the creek or at times of rain), seeing that they bathed, attending to any minor wounds they acquired, and controlling their mischievous behavior. Another responsibility was remaining patient with the children.

The first sentence says simply what it has to say. The second sentence starts to sound like a report. It strives for a needless explicitness ("on several occasions") and it aims for a pseudo-scientific neutrality of description, "the negative aspects of fighting." To remain on the same stylistic level as the first sentence, it ought to read, "So, I often told them to stop." "Other responsibilities included" is the language of a job description. The frantic scramble for a summer camp is being viewed through a personnel form. The prose is scary as well as stilted because life has been reduced to something that will fit in a file cabinet. Only on official forms do small boys "acquire minor wounds" or counselors "attend" them. In life, they cut themselves and you give them a Band-Aid. In life, you keep them out of the creek and out of the rain, instead of "keeping them dry (when near the creek or at times of rain)." And, instead of "controlling their mischievous behavior," you make them behave or even give them a kick in the pants. As for "Another responsibility was remaining patient with children," that translates into, "I had to keep my temper." If the writer had stayed on the low-style level he began with, he would have written:

> Twelve-year-old boys like to fight. Often, I had to stop them. And I had to keep them out of the rain, and the creek, and mischief generally. I had to give out Band-Aids and keep my temper.

Why didn't he? You don't write the Official Style by nature. It has to be learned. Why did he fall into it here? *He was applying for something.* And you apply for something—in this case, admission to medical school—on a form. And a form requires an official style. The Official Style. It makes what you've done sound important and, still more important than important, *official.*

Ever since George Orwell's famous essay "Politics and the English Language" (1946), the Official Style has been interpreted as a vast conspiracy to soften our minds and corrupt our political judgment. Social science jargon has been seen as pure hokum, an attempt to seem more scientific than you are. And the language of the Pentagon and Dow Chemical bureaucrats during the Vietnam War often seemed to combine the worst of these two worlds. The Orwell conspiracy theory is sometimes true, but not the whole truth. We all want to fit in, to talk the language of the country. This desire is what keeps society glued together. So the impulses that attract us to the Official Style are not always perverse or depraved. Just the opposite. They are the primary social impulses. And so when we analyze the Official Style, we're really talking about how we live now, about our *society* as well as our prose, about how to survive in the System. What does the prose tell us about the society?

Well, it is a euphemistic society, for a start. It thinks of every town dump as a "Sanitary Landfill Site," every mentally retarded child as "exceptional," every dog catcher as an "animal welfare officer," every pig pen as a "unitary hog-raising facility." Society may have its pains and problems, but language can sugarcoat them. An Official Stylist would never say that an area was so polluted plants obviously couldn't grow there. Instead: "Natural biotic habitats are conspicuously absent from the region."

The second rule in this society is "Keep your head down. Don't assert anything you'll have to take the blame for. Don't, if you can help it, assert anything at all." Anthony Sampson, in his *Anatomy of Britain,* has culled a few examples of this supercaution from a British Civil Service version of the Official Style and supplied plain language translations.

We hope that it is fully appreciated that . . .
 You completely fail to realize that . . .

Greater emphasis should be laid on . . .
 You haven't bothered to notice . . .

We have the impression that insufficient study has been given to . . .
 No one has considered . . .

Our enquiry seemed to provide a welcome opportunity for discussions of problems of this kind . . .
 No one had thought of that before . . .

We do not think that there is sufficient awareness . . .
 There is ignorance . . .

There has been a tendency in the past to overestimate the possibilities of useful short-term action in public investment . . .
 You should look ahead . . .

There should be an improvement in the arrangements to enable ministers to discharge their collective responsibility
 . . .
 The cabinet should work together . . .

(Anatomy of Britain, New York: Harper & Row, 1962)

The main rule is clear. Don't make an assertion you can get tagged with later. It may come back to haunt you. So never write "I think" or "I did." Keep the verbs passive and impersonal: "It was concluded that" or "appropriate action was initiated on the basis of systematic discussion indicating that." Often, as with politicians being interviewed on TV, the Official Style aims deliberately at saying nothing at all, but saying it in the required way. Or at saying the obvious in a seemingly impressive way. The official stylist must seem in control of everything but responsible for nothing. Thus a congressman, instead of saying that the government will listen to consumer complaints, says that it will "review existing mechanisms of consumer input, thruput, and output and seek ways of improving these linkages via consumer consumption channels." The computer language of input, output, and interface has been seized upon by the Official Style as a kind of poetic diction, a body of sacred and intrinsically beautiful metaphors. Thus, a U.S. Senator indicted on bribery charges does not ask the advice of his friends. Instead, bathing in computer charisma, he is "currently receiving personal and political input from my supporters and friends throughout the state."

It is often hard to tell with the Official Style how much is self-conscious put-on and how much is real ineptitude, genuine system-sickness. Students often say that the length and physical weight of their papers is more important than what they say, yet it is not only in school that papers are graded thus. Here is a famous Washington lawyer, talking about legal language:

> In these days when every other type of professional report, good or poor, is dressed up in a lovely ringed and colored plastic binder, some people still are prone to judge legal performance quantitatively by verbal volume. Thirty years ago two of us answered a difficult and intricate legal problem by concisely writing: "Gentlemen, after examining the statute in your state, all analogous statutes, and all of the cases, we have concluded that what you want to do is lawful." That client was not happy; he went down to Wall Street, got the same opinion backed by thirty turgid typewritten pages, and felt much more comfortable.
>
> (Quoted in Joseph C. Guelden's *The Superlawyers*)

It is not only bureaucrats who find length and obscurity impressive.

Here is another example of the Official Style inflating something short and sweet:

> A policy decision inexorably enforced upon a depression-prone individual whose posture in respect to his total

psychophysical environment is rendered antagonistic by apprehension or by inner-motivated disinclination for ongoing participation in human existence is the necessity for effectuating a positve selection between two alternative programs of action, namely, (a) the continuance of the above-mentioned existence irrespective of the dislocations, dissatisfactions, and disabilities incurred in such a mode, or (b) the voluntary termination of such existence by self-initiated instrumentality, irrespective in this instance of the undetermined character of the subsequent environment, if any, in which the subject may be positioned as an end result of this irrevocable determination.

Serious or a joke? A joke. In fact, one of the clever variations on common clichés by Richard D. Altick in *A Preface to Critical Reading* to illustrate the Official Style. The text varied is, of course, "To be or not be, that is the question."

Now, by contrast, someone genuinely system-sick. No joke. He has come to *think* in the Official Style. The librarian of a large library, in a very large bureaucracy, is trying to tell us that some books will be kept behind the desk, others put on shelves outside:

Primarily, this reorganization and the related changes are designed to facilitate the processing of lists. Placing responsibility for the processing of lists directly within the Technical Processing Division will provide a smoother and more efficient work flow, which we anticipate will result in your materials becoming more readily available. Second, it will allow optimum access to the collection, and third, provide a browsing capability formerly denied users of reserved materials.

For this new system to be successful we need your full cooperation. The attached Guidelines for Reserve Lists details the manner in which we need lists prepared. Essentially, we are requesting that required readings be distinguished from optional readings. Required readings stipulated for two-hour use will be placed on closed reserve in

65

an area behind the circulation desk. Required readings circulating for one day will remain in the open stacks; however, as opposed to regular open stack materials, these books will be marked to indicate one day use. Optional readings will circulate for regular loan periods.

In the past, the primary means for soliciting faculty input for acquiring materials for the College Library has been through reserve lists. It is our desire that optimal reading lists for undergraduates will be an effective mechanism for faculty to identify materials for the library's open stack collection.

It is our hope that you will find these changes mutually beneficial for yourselves and your students.

Your cooperation and assistance in this matter will be greatly appreciated.

If he translated this into language less wordy, shapeless, pompous, and pretentious, he might make things clearer to the faculty but he would be only a librarian, not a bureaucratic witch doctor. He would be simply putting the books out on the shelf, not "providing a browsing capability." Try a revision of your own in this spirit.

You must, if you are to write prose in an America and a world fated to become ever more bureaucratic, learn how to use the Official Style, even perhaps how to enjoy it, without becoming imprisoned by it. You must manage to remember who is on first base, even if often you will not want to let on that you know.

Long ago, La Rochefoucauld talked about a grave manner as "a mysterious carriage of the body to cover defects of the mind." The Official Style has elevated this into an article of faith. Here is a sociological sample collected by Malcolm Cowley, with his translation:

In effect, it was hypothesized that certain physical data categories including housing types and densities, land use characteristics, and ecological location constitute a scalable content area. This could be called a continuum of residential desirability. Likewise, it was hypothesized that several social data categories, describing the same census tracts, and referring generally to the social stratification system of the city, would also be scalable. This scale would be called a continuum of socio-economic status. Thirdly, it was hypothesized that there would be a high positive correlation between the scale types on each continuum.

Here's the translation:

Rich people live in big houses set further apart than those of poor people. By looking at an aerial photograph of any American city, we can distinguish the richer from the poorer neighborhoods.

("Sociological Habit Patterns in Linguistic Transmogrification," *The Reporter,* September 20, 1956)

Such prose seems to aim at being scientific but actually wants to be priestly, to cast a witch doctor's spell. To translate the prose into a plain style—that is, to revise it into ordinary English—breaks the spell and defeats the purpose.

We face, then, the euphemistic habit yet again, though on a larger scale. The Official Style always wants to make things seem better than they are, more mysterious and yet somehow more controlled, more inevitable. It strives, at all times, both to disarm and to impress us. It suggests that it sees the world differently—sees, even, a different world. It suggests that those who see in this way form a happy band of brothers. Now such a use of language does not, to students of literature, sound unfamiliar. It is called *poetic diction.* And this is what the Official Style amounts to—a kind of poetic diction. Here we come to the central problem with the Official Style. There is no point in reproaching it for not being clear. It does not really want to be clear. It wants to be *poetic.* At its best, it wants to tell you how it *feels* to be an official, to project the sense of numinous self-importance officialdom confers. It wants to make a prosaic world mysterious.

I know, I know. It doesn't do it very well. But that's not

the point. Until we see what it is trying to do, we can neither understand it nor translate it with any pleasure. Maybe a comparison from another time and context will make the point clearer. Here is a series of plain language translations of Official Style poetic diction that the English poet Alexander Pope compiled for a satire on false poetic sublimity called *Peri Bathos* (1728). He gives first the poetic diction and then the ordinary language equivalent.

Poetic Diction	Plain English
For whom thus rudely pleads my loud-tongued gate That he may enter? . . .	Who knocks at the Door?
Advance the fringed curtains of thy eyes, And tell me who comes yonder . . .	See who is there.
The wooden guardian of our privacy Quick on its axle turn . . .	Shut the Door.
Bring me what Nature, tailor to the *Bear* To *Man* himself denied: She gave me Cold But would not give me Clothes . . .	Bring my Clothes.
Bring forth some remnant of the *Promethean* theft, Quick to expand th' inclement air congealed By *Boreas'* rude breath . . .	Light the Fire.

Poetic Diction	Plain English
Yon Luminary amputation needs, Thus shall you save its half-extinguished life.	Snuff the Candle.
Apply thine engine to the spongy door, Set *Bacchus* from his glassy prison free, And strip white *Ceres* of her nut-brown coat.	Uncork the Bottle, and cut the Bread.

And here is a modern version of such a list, culled from an Environmental Impact Statement filed by the FAA.

Poetic Diction	Plain English
"limited in length"	short
"small faunal species"	rats
"experience growth"	grow
"annoyance factors"	annoyances
"police protection services"	police
"aircraft with lower noise emission characteristics"	quieter planes
"overlain by impervious surfaces"	paved
"exotic effluents"	chemicals
"weedy species"	weeds
"stepwise methodology"	method
"pollutant emissions control strategies"	smog filters
"olfactory impact"	smell

Here is yet another glossary, an unintentional self-satire this time, issued by the U.S. Office of Education (1971).

69

Poetic Diction	**Plain English**
Allocation of personnel and logistic resources to accomplish an identifiable objective. Activities constitute the basis for defining personnel assignments and for scheduling system operations.	Activity
The splitting of an entity into its constituent parts and the determination of relations among the parts and groups of the components.	Analysis
Production and refinement of a system or a product through trial-revision until it accomplishes its specified objectives.	Development
Those things (actions) that must be done to accomplish the overall job are referred to as functions.	Functions
To carry out. To fulfill. To give practical effect to and ensure of actual fulfillment by concrete measures.	Implement
Enhanced performance on any important dimension without detriment to the other essential dimensions.	Improvement
The job to be done, be it a product, a completed service, or a change in the condition of something or somebody.	Mission
A discrepancy or differential between "what is" and "what should be" (i.e., "what is required" or "what is desired"). In educational planning, "need" refers to problems rather than solutions,	Need

Poetic Diction	Plain English
to the student "product" rather than to the resources for achieving that product, to the ends of education rather than to the means for attaining those ends.	
That toward which effort is directed. An intent statement and production for which a procedure is developed and resources allocated with a specific time frame and a measurable product signaling attainment.	Objectives
The organizational, procedural, technological, and support arrangements by which an agency has the capacity to apply problem-solving processes to any problem that it may face.	Planning Capability or Planning Competence
Elements of a function that, when performed by people and things in proper sequential order, will or should resolve the parent function. Tasks may be performed by people, equipment, or people/equipment combination.	Tasks

(Robert A. Watson, "Making Things Perfectly Clear," *Saturday Review*, July 24, 1971).

This bureaucratic glossary was issued in the name of clarity but aims obviously at something else entirely, at a playful, poetic, ornamental use of language. Those who use the Official Style seldom acknowledge the paradox, but you must learn to see it if you are not to make grotesque mistakes. Clarity is often the last thing the Official Style really wants to create and, if you find yourself in a bureaucratic context, often the last thing *you* want to create. If you are writing a government memo, a sociological report, or a grant proposal in education, writing it in plain English could be disastrous. You

71

may well want, in marshaling your thoughts, to write out an ordinary language version. But you must then translate it into the Official Style. You must, that is, learn to read, write, and translate the Official Style as if it were a foreign language. Play games with it by all means, but don't get fooled by it.

Bureaucrats have, in the last few years, begun to do just this—play games with it. One government official, Philip Broughton, created something called the "Systematic Buzz Phrase Projector." It consists of three columns of words:

Column 1	Column 2	Column 3
0. integrated	0. management	0. options
1. total	1. organizational	1. flexibility
2. systematized	2. monitored	2. capability
3. parallel	3. reciprocal	3. mobility
4. functional	4. digital	4. programming
5. responsive	5. logistical	5. concept
6. optional	6. transitional	6. time-phase
7. synchronized	7. incremental	7. projection
8. compatible	8. third-genera-	8. hardware
9. balanced	tion	9. contingency
	9. policy	

(*Newsweek,* May 6, 1968)

You think of any three numbers, 747 say, and then read off the corresponding words, "synchronized digital projection." It is a device to generate verbal ornament, a machine for poetic diction. Try making up a version for whatever dialect of the Official Style you need to write—governmental, sociological, educational, or psychoanalytic. Not only will it lend new resonance and authority to your prose, it will act as a multiplier, increasing length and weight. It also acts as a mechanical muse, generates inspiration, or at least serviceable instant flapdoodle. Produce a phrase by the three-number procedure, invent a sentence for it, and then spend a paragraph or two reflecting on what it might mean. Invent a reality to which the phrase can refer.

Let's run over the basic elements of the Official Style again. (1) It is built on *nouns,* vague, general nouns. These nouns are

72

usually of Latin derivation, "shun" words like fixa*tion*, func-*tion*, construc*tion*, educa*tion*, organiza*tion*. (2) These nouns are often, as in the game, modified by adjectives made up from other nouns like them, as in "incremental throughput" or "functional input." (3) All action is passive and impersonal. No active intransitive verbs and no direct objects. Never "I decided to fire him" but "It has been determined that the individual's continued presence in the present personnel con-figuration would tend to be to the detriment of the ongoing operational efficiency of the organizational unit in which the individual is currently employed." (4) Nothing is called by its ordinary name. You don't decide to bomb a town; instead, "It has been determined to maintain an aggressive and opera-tional attack posture." You don't set up an office, you "initiate an ongoing administrative facility." (5) The status quo is preserved in syntax. All motion is converted into stasis. The Official Style denies, as much as possible, the reality of action. You don't dislike someone, you "maintain a posture of disapproval toward" him. You don't decide to hire someone, you "initiate the hiring process." Above all, you make the simple sound complex, as in the following prizewinner.

Official Style

The purpose of this project is to develop the capability for institutions of higher learning and community agencies and organizations to coalesce for the development of community services that would maximize the available resources from a number of institutions and provide communication and priority needs and the responses of the educational needs of a given community.

Plain English

This project aims to teach universities and community organizations how to work more efficiently together.

Already you can see the problem. The plain English sounds *too* simple. A worthy project, no doubt, but who would ever *fund* anything as obvious as that?

Official Style prose often grows from a need to say something—to a TV camera, for example—when nothing, or at least nothing candid, can be said. So when a State Department spokesman is asked how the Conference is going, he does not say "God knows!" but instead:

I think it is already possible that this particular summit is one that is on the way to a substantial result. There has been evidence of an encouragingly large area of agreement toward a concrete and concerted action program by the various countries represented here—a program that will be concise and meaningful in its nature.

Maybe only the old-fashioned crooks could afford to be candid, but such candor certainly sounds refreshing to our bureaucratized ears. Listen to Al Capone speaking to the press:

I make my money by supplying a public demand. If I break the law, my customers, who number hundreds of the best people in Chicago, are as guilty as I am. The only difference between us is that I sell and they buy. Everybody calls me a racketeer. I call myself a business man. When I sell liquor, it's bootlegging. When my patrons serve it on a silver tray on Lake Shore Drive, it's hospitality.

Notice how easily this passage can be read aloud? How carefully a pattern of balance is built up?

If I break the law	my customers are as guilty as I

74

I sell	they buy
I call myself a businessman	Everybody calls me a racketeer
I sell liquor, it's bootlegging	my patrons serve it, it's hospitality

He wants you to find the pattern of his thought, not love it.

Sometimes, though, the Official Stylist is not mendacious, or even self-important, but simply absent in mind. He can write the Official Style from knee-jerk habit, like the galvanic twitch of a laboratory frog after its brain has been removed. So here, an urban planner:

> The current design process was discussed and found lacking because there is no recognized programming phase; the architect is not often party to fundamental planning decisions concerning alternatives to building; the user is not a participant in design discussions. There is no behavioral design methodology, nor are there statements of accountability for decisions made, and there is no feedback mechanism or information clearinghouse. The need for a more comprehensive design process is immediate. The Behavioral Design Process is presented below in some detail as a guide to implementation of a user-oriented design methodology.

The writer is trying to say something simple but important. Into plain English, a sentence at a time, with the help of the Paramedic Method:

ORIGINAL

> The current design process was discussed and found lacking because there is no recognized programming phase; (16 words)

75

REVISION

Current design lacks a programming phase; (6 words; LF 63%)

ORIGINAL

. . . the architect is not often party to fundamental planning decisions concerning alternatives to building; the user is not a participant in design discussions. (23 words)

REVISION

. . . Neither architect nor tenant participates in fundamental planning decisions. (9 words; LF 61%)

ORIGINAL

There is no behavioral design methodology, nor are there statements of accountability for decisions made, and there is no feedback mechanism or information clearinghouse. The need for a more comprehensive design process is immediate. (34 words)

REVISION

We badly need a system that allows a designer to meet the people who will live in his design, and to learn their wishes and consider their needs. (28 words; LF 18%)

ORIGINAL

The Behavioral Design Process is presented below in some detail as a guide to implementation of a user-oriented design methodology. (21 words)

REVISION

Behavioral Design, as presented below, shows how this could be done. (11 words; LF 47%)

Now, the entire *original:*

The current design process was discussed and found lacking because there is no recognized programming phase; the architect is not often party to fundamental planning decisions concerning alternatives to building; the user is not a participant in design discussions. There is no behavioral design methodology, nor are there statements of accountability for decisions made, and there is no feedback mechanism or information clearinghouse. The need for a more comprehensive design process is immediate. The Behavioral Design Process is presented below in some detail as a guide to implementation of a user-oriented design methodology. (94 words)

And the *revision:*

Current design lacks a programming phase; neither architect nor tenant participates in fundamental planning decisions. We badly need a system that allows a designer to meet the people who will live in his design, to learn their wishes and consider their needs. Behavioral Design, as presented below, shows how this could be done. (52 words; LF 45%)

But if buildings should be designed for people, shouldn't prose styles be too? The Official Style, often, is not. It tries to stall people, confuse them, shut them out. It deliberately hides the ball. Look at this example of the Official Style at its most antisocial. It comes from an Environmental Impact Statement that discusses the effects of jet noise on the people who live around an urban airport.

The findings of ongoing research have shown that a number of physiological effects occur under conditions of noise exposure. . . . These studies demonstrate that noise exposure does influence bodily changes, such as the so-called vegetative functions, by inhibition of gastric juices, lowered skin resistance, modified pulse rate and increased metabolism. . . .

77

Other studies have investigated the generalized physiological effects of noise in relation to cardiovascular disturbances, gastrointestinal problems, impairment of performance on motor tracking tasks and vascular disturbances, as well as various physical ailments. Miller (1974) states that, "Steady noise of 90 dB increases tension in all muscles." Welch (1972) concludes that "environmental sound has all-pervasive effects on the body, influencing virtually every organ system and function that has been studied," and Cohen (1971) summarized that "the distressing effects of noise alone or combined with other stress factors can eventually overwhelm man's capability for healthy adjustment with resultant physical or mental ailments. . . ."

The survey determined the presence of annoyance reactions which have been identified as indicators of stressful response to environmental noise among respondents both inside and outside the noise impact area. . . .

No need to do a detailed analysis at this stage of the game—the formula as before. In this distanced and impersonal world, no one ever suffers; they experience "the presence of annoyance reactions." And, in the report's ever-cautious style it only "appears" that the airport produces such reactions among residents.

Human beings, we need to remind ourselves here, are social beings. Our reality is a social reality. Our identity draws its felt life from our relation to other people. We become uneasy if, for extended periods of time, we neither hear nor see other people. We feel uneasy with the Official Style for the same reason. It has no human voice, no face, no personality behind it. It creates no society, encourages no social conversation. We feel that it is *unreal*. And, the "better" it is, the more true-to-type, the more unreal it becomes.

But public prose need not erase human reality. It can do just the opposite, as in the following passage from the same airport controversy—a letter from a homeowners' group president. With it, we return to human life.

78

Our Homeowners Association was formed about a year and a half ago principally because of an overwhelming fear of what might happen to our homes, schools and community as a result of any steps which might be taken by Lockheed and/or the City of Burbank. Our community is inexorably linked to Hollywood-Burbank Airport. The northern part of the North/South runway is in our city. . . .

Our community consists of a vast majority of single-family residences, and long-time owners with "paid in full" or "almost paid up" mortgages. We have been told, "You moved in next to the airport, it was there before you were." This is true in most cases. But, and this is a big "but"—it was an entirely different airport when most of us moved into the area. 20 to 25 years ago, the airport was "home" to small planes. We actually enjoyed watching them buzz around, and many of us spent Sunday afternoons at the airport while our children were amused watching the little planes. However, the advent of the jet plane at HBA changed the entire picture. Suddenly we were the neighbors of a Noise Factory! . . .

Our children are bombarded with noise in 2 local elementary schools, Roscoe and Glenwood. Teachers have to stop teaching until the noise passes over and everyone waits "for the next one." If the school audiometrist wants an in-depth test for a child with questionable hearing, the child must be taken away from the school altogether to eliminate outside noises.

Our backyards, streets, parks and churches, too, are inundated with noise . . . noise is an ever-constant fact of life for us. There is seldom a time when one cannot hear a plane somewhere in the vicinity—it may be "up" or it may be "down," but once a motor is turned on, we hear it!

We might well be asked, "Why do you continue to live in such a place?" Put in plain and simple terms—we have no place else to go! Years have passed and we have put more money into our mortgages and into our property.

79

We have developed long-time friendships with neighbors and the Community. We don't want to move! . . .

Where do we go? Who is going to pay us—and how much will we be paid—for being uprooted? Who sets the price on losing a street and an entire neighborhood full of long-time friends? If 7 schools are to be closed, where do the children go? What happens to the faculty and staff at the schools? The parochial schools? The small business man who sells consumer goods—what happens when there is no one to sell to?

Plain English, in such a context, takes on almost the moral grandeur of the high style. The language of ordinary life reasserts our common humanity. Precisely the humanity, we have now come to see, the Official Style so often seeks to banish. It is a bad style, then, when it denatures human relations. When we consider that it is becoming the accepted language for the organizations that govern human relations, we can begin to see how stylistic and moral issues converge. To that convergence the following two chapters now turn.

CHAPTER 5

The Perils of Revision

Macpherson v. Texas Department of Water Resources

It is much easier to revise prose in a classroom or a textbook than on the job; no context qualifies your red pencil. When you are actually doing business, things are rarely so simple. The memo you are revising was written by your boss, or by a touchy but valuable subordinate. Or a customer. Or a competitor. The social and political situation governs what you can and what you want to do. The bigger the organization, the more complex the social situation in which writing occurs. Big corporations and government bureaus often have style sheets, publicly proclaimed definitions of "good prose," as well as many tacit but strong conventions. You must obey them. Often you want simply to remain anonymous. When I was drafted into the Army a friend who had been there counselled me to find the biggest group I could and jump right in the middle of it. Good advice, and not only for the Army. Often an itch for survival will blend you right into the woodwork. If people in that woodwork write the Official Style, you had better facilitate your prose utilization in the same way. If you want to get a contract from the Bureau of Naval Ordinance, you'll write the kind of language they understand there.

But, as we saw in the last chapter, there are good reasons to avoid the Official Style when you can. You'll save your company some time and money more likely than not, and often a good deal of trouble as well. You must remember, though, that writing is a very "love me, love my dog" personal kind of thing. It represents the public self of the writer and you must treat it accordingly. In the short drama of revision that we will explore in this chapter—*"Macpherson v. Texas Department of Water Resources"*—Ms. Macpherson forgot this cardinal rule and lost her job for it. The incident took place in a government agency rather than in business, but the lessons of writing and management that it teaches are so apropos to business writing that we are going to conclude our prose revision labors by studying it in detail. It richly repays such study. Here is the case as reported by the Appellate Court. It provides a brilliant object lesson in the relationships between prose style and political power; shows, that is to say, business writing in its natural habitat.

MACPHERSON v. DEPT OF WATER RESOURCES

U.S. Court of Appeals,
Fifth Circuit (New Orleans)

MACPHERSON v. TEXAS DEPARTMENT OF WATER RESOURCES, et al., No. 83-1692, June 25, 1984

CIVIL RIGHTS ACT OF 1964
  Sex   Discharge   108.4112
      108.8101

Finding that state agency discharged female employee because of her pertness in appending to memorandum specific and general comments designed to inform its author of his literary ineptitude and in then sending memorandum back to executive director, who originally sent memorandum over his signature, and not because of her gender is not clearly erroneous, where evidence supports conclusion that final decision to discharge the reviser was made before director discovered that female employee, who had received more promotions and merit raises than any other employee in her section, was the reviser.

Appeal from the U.S. District Court for the Western District of Texas. Affirmed.

Leonard J. Schwartz and Katherine L. Moore (Waterman & Schwartz), Austin, Tex., for appellant.

Jim Mattox, Attorney General of Texas, and Evelyn S. Tatum, Assistant Attorney General, for appellee.

Before GEE, POLITZ, and JOHNSON, Circuit Judges.

Full Text of Opinion

GEE, Circuit Judge:—This appeal concerns whether Ms. Gwendolyn Macpherson was dismissed from her position with an agency of the State of Texas for a wrong reason: being female. In a bench trial, the court gave judgment for the defendant, entering detailed findings of fact and conclusions of law. On the peculiar facts of the case, we conclude that one of his findings—which is supported by the record evidence—is dispositive, so that we need not look beyond it to affirm.

The record indicates that Ms. Macpherson is a graduate geologist of high intelligence, independent mind and—one may infer—somewhat venturesome spirit. Employed by a predecessor department of the defendant agency in March 1976, she established an enviable work record, marred by only a single verbal reprimand for climbing a fence to examine certain deposits on private property without obtaining the landowner's permission. During her brief tenure with the state, she received more promotions and merit raises than any other employee in her section.

In September 1977, her department was merged with two other state water agencies to become the present defendant agency and defendant Harvey Davis became executive director of the new entity. One may infer from the record that in the months immediately following the merger Davis was strained by the inevitable tensions consequent to his new position and the effort to harmonize his amalgamated charges into a functional entity.

In January 1978, Mr. Davis circulated a memorandum over his signature to his division directors within the agency. The memo had actually been prepared by a staff attorney and was entitled "Outside Requests of [sic] Staff Testimony at Administrative and Judicial Hearings." Like the title, portions of it were poorly worded. Ms. Macpherson determined that it required grammatical and stylistic improvement. She therefore proceeded to correct Mr. Davis's memo in searching detail, appending both specific and general comments calculated to bring home to the author his literary ineptitude. Her final observation fairly gives the flavor of the whole:

> You frequently leave out articles (a, an, the) in front of nouns. You tend to obfuscate by using long, unwieldy phraseology. Simplify! Simplify! This will help correct your tendency to misplace modifiers. The content of this memo is confusing. It is obvious to me that when one is subpoenaed one must appear, regardless of the opinion of the Department. Furthermore, one must tell the truth when under oath.
>
> Please rewrite and resubmit.[1]

She then anonymously mailed her revision to Mr. Davis in an envelope marked "Personal," and thus it came directly to his hand.

[1]The memo and Ms. Macpherson's corrections and comments are reproduced in full at the foot of our opinion.

While adhering to the ceiling of his office, revised memo in hand, Mr. Davis determined to fire the reviser, whomever he or she might be. As the trial court chastely put it in Finding of Fact No. 16, "The termination decision was made prior to the discovery of the identity of the employee who revised the memo and anonymously sent it to Mr. Harvey Davis." After an investigation in the course of which she readily admitted the revision and anonymous return of the memo,[2] and a meeting between Mr. Davis and the director of Ms. Macpherson's division, her immediate supervisor, and the agency general counsel, Davis reiterated his decision that the reviser, her identity now known, should be dismissed and she was.

As we note above, the trial court, to whose opportunity to hear and view the witnesses we must defer, concluded that a final decision to discharge the reviser was made before her identity became known. The record contains evidence that supports this finding, as well as evidence tending to support a determination that the initial decision was tentative and became final only after she was discovered. It is not for us, however, to second-guess the trial court's credibility choices among differing pieces of testimony—even those coming from the same witness or witnesses—unless a review of the record leaves us "with the definite and firm conviction that a mistake has been committed." United States v. United States Gypsum Co., 333 U.S. 364, 395, 68 S.Ct. 525, 92 L.Ed. 746 (1948), reh'g denied, 333 U.S. 869, 68 S.Ct. 788, 92 L.Ed. 1147. That is not the case today, and the finding must stand.

Since the decision to fire Ms. Macpherson was taken when her identity, and perforce her gender, were un-

---

[2]Adding, according to the testimony of her immediate supervisor, that "she just could not stand the idea that an Executive Director of an agency like that putting out a memo that was in such bad form grammatically and that something to the effect that she really didn't like to work for anybody like that." (Tr. 135).

known and merely carried out after they were discovered, there can be no question of sex discrimination on this record. There it ends.

In closing, we observe that although the unique facts of today's case lend themselves irresistibly to somewhat ironic treatment, we do not view lightly the small bureaucratic tragedy that the record reveals: a harried executive has lost his temper and a valuable—if somewhat pert—state employee has lost her position. On this record, however, we cannot hold the trial judge clearly erroneous in finding that it was Ms. Macpherson's pertness and not her gender that cost her the job she held. We do not sit to revise employment decisions taken hastily or for insufficient reasons, only those taken for illegal ones. And so, with all sympathy and good wishes for the future of Ms. Macpherson, we conclude that the trial court's judgment must be

AFFIRMED.[3]

Let's begin by looking at the original memo, as annotated by Ms. Macpherson, which caused all the trouble. It begins, as do all memos, with a schematic heading:

TO: All Division Directors

THRU:

FROM: Harvey Davis, Executive Director

SUBJECT: Outside Requests of Staff Testimony at Administrative and Judicial Hearings

All very boring formulaic stuff, it seems. But what is really going in this—or any—memo heading? What do you learn from it as a reader? What constraints does it impose upon you as a writer? First, the routing instructions define your audi-

---

[3]In anticipation of a critical review of our remarks, we have been at some pains with their style and grammar.

Texas Department of Water Resources

INTEROFFICE MEMORANDUM

TO   :   All Division Directors   DATE: January 16, 1978

THRU   :

FROM   .   Harvey Davis, Executive Director

SUBJECT: Outside Requests of Staff Testimony at Administrative and
           Judicial Hearings

Section 5.173 of the Texas Water Code provides:

> "[the] position of and information developed by the department shall
> be presented by the executive director or his designated representative
> at hearings of the board and the commission and at hearings held by
> federal, state, and local agencies on matters affecting the public's
> interest in the state's water resources, including matters that have
> been determined to be policies of the state. The executive director
> shall be named a party in hearings before the commission."

The position of the Executive Director is developed during application review by
legal and technical staff and formalized prior to submission of the application
and the recommendation of the Executive Director to the Commission for setting
of a contested APA hearing. Obviously, disagreements will arise among a
professional staff on the position that should be taken. However, absent the
development of previously unknown information during the hearing process
which materially affects the recommendation, each representative is expected
to advocate the position taken.

Occasionally, other parties to a hearing will seek the testimony of Department
employees, either because of general expertise or because of knowledge relating
to an application developed in the review process. Any employee of the Department who is requested or subpoenaed to appear to present testimony at any public
hearing, administrative or judicial, relative to his official duties with the
agency must immediately notify the Executive Director of such request upon receipt.
We will then be able to review the request with ample time to determine a course
of action. All employees who testify in public hearings, whether called on
behalf of the Executive Director or by another party, are expected to fully
and truthfully answer all questions.

87

All Division Directors   -2-   January 16, 1978

In general, upon request from an outside person, the Department will provide the expert witness on state time and at state expense to impartially provide information to the judge or examiner, rather than to allow a litigant to call a Department employee as his witness. The refusal of employee's acceptance of witness fees and travel expenses, even where provided by law, will help insure impartiality. However, a case by case determination of utilization of State travel monies will be made by this Office to insure the reasonableness of the request in light of the requested employee's expertise and the relation of the subject of the lawsuit to the statutory responsibilities of the Department.

Harvey Davis

Harvey Davis

What request?

This is the first time a lawsuit has been mentioned. I thought this memo concerned public hearings.

Overall comments

You frequently leave out articles (a, an, the) in front of nouns.
You tend to obfuscate by using long, unwieldly phraseology. Simplify!
Simplify! This will help correct your tendency to misplace modifiers.
The content of this memo is confusing. It is obvious to me that when one is subpoenaed one must appear, regardless of the opinion of the Department.
Furthermore, one must tell the truth when under oath.

Please rewrite and resubmit.

ence for you, and much more explicitly than writers can usually know. Here is your readership. Of course others may come to read it (it is directed to Division Directors and Ms. Macpherson was not, so far as we know, a Division Director), but the target audience is *fully known.* For the writer, this will make many decisions for you—tone, stylistic level, length, and so on. And for the reader, you will know *how to read* the memo; its *genre,* or literary type, will have been defined for you. You'll know with what kind of salt to take it. Harvey Davis was a senior boss, a boss of bosses, an Executive Director. That tells you a lot. He was also new on the job, and that tells you a lot more. He may not know his audience, after all, very well, even though he knows who they are. That will have to wait upon experience in the job. But he clearly writes from a position of power; that position will form part of any response to the memo. No reader can pretend not to know *who wrote it.* The SUBJECT heading conveys two very different kinds of messages. On the surface, it tells us the subject of the memo: "Outside Requests of Staff Testimony at Administrative and Judicial Hearings." Beneath the surface, it casts grave doubt on the writer's linguistic competence. The writer means "Outside Requests *for* Staff Testimony." Someone is requesting the staff members to testify. But he doesn't say that. Instead, he makes a mistake in English idiom, using a nonidiomatic preposition, "of," to mean "for." A trifling mistake, though, like mistaking "disinterested" for "uninterested"? Not at all. To make a mistake in idiom means you don't dwell in the family of native English speakers. It is a very small but *very* revealing error. It puts you outside a very large but *very* important group. Like a mistake in manners, it affects the observer out of all proportion to its intrinsic importance. (It does make a difference, of course, since it means something different from what the writer intends it to mean, but enough redundancy is built into the message so we can see around the mistake.) The writer has lost his authority before he has begun. He has put himself in the penalty box, labelled "to be corrected." Ms.

Macpherson did not, as it happens, correct this error, but she is alert to errors of idiomatic preposition, for she corrects one later on, an incorrect "of" is changed to an idiomatic "about." The mistake in the heading establishes her role vis-à-vis the writer, a role strongly at odds with the boss-subordinate one. Smart subordinates don't fall into this trap, but smart bosses don't set it either.

Now, before we look at the memo in detail, stand back from it and look at it *cum commento,* with all its marginal annotations. What does it remind you of? That's right. One of those papers you wrote in Freshman English. Ms. Macpherson removes the memo from its original dramatic context and puts it in another play, one in which she is the teacher and good old Harv Davis finds himself sitting in the corner wearing a dunce cap. It is this reversal that makes him hit the ceiling and fire her on the spot, not what she says about his prose. He does not sit down and ponder his mistakes in nonidiomatic prepositions, lament, or vaunt, misplacing his modifier. He responds not to a prose revision but to the power reversal that it implies. This reversal is implied, to one degree or another, by every act of revision and none of us should ever forget it. School teachers often do for, after all, we are the ones in power and so don't feel threatened. Revising prose is first, and often foremost, an act of political power. Forget this and you may, like Ms. Macpherson, find yourself out of a job.

Her comments, questions, and corrections are, with a couple of exceptions, sensible and helpful. They are also, with no exceptions, insufferably school-teacherish and superior in tone. The concluding comment—that great occasion for displays of professorial humor—takes the cake:

> You frequently leave out articles (a, an, the) in front of nouns. [Again, the revealing errors in English idiom.] You tend to obfuscate by using long, unwieldy phraseology. Simplify! This will help correct your tendency to misplace modifiers. The content of this memo is confusing. It is

obvious to me [note the stress on "to me"?] that when one is subpoenaed one must appear, regardless of the opinion of the Department. Furthermore, one must tell the truth when under oath. Please rewrite and resubmit.

Zowie! The tonal coloration accompanying this bracing criticism goes something like, "Boss, you really are a long-winded, semiliterate, lazy jerk. Try it again and try, if you can, to get it right this time." Ms. Macpherson was an exemplary employee in every other way. Could she have been this naive? Well, maybe not. Maybe she expected Davis to read the correction ironically, as a kind of laughing invocation of the teacher-pupil relationship to call attention to some (as we shall see later) very serious mistakes. Or maybe she just expected him to be sensible enough, and self-controlled enough, to accept the criticism for what it was worth (again, a lot, as it turns out) and ignore the tone. Or at least to find out who wrote it, and thus perhaps why, before acting. Ms. Macpherson's supervisor testified that Ms. Macpherson "just could not stand the idea that an Executive Director of an agency like that putting out a memo that was in such bad form grammatically and . . . that she did not really like to work for anybody like that." If so, she got her wish. But perhaps she thought that any sensible manager would call a subordinate in and set the power relation straight in private. After all, Ms. Macpherson had sent the message marked "Personal" (the Judge misses the point of this in his comment upon it) so that no one else would see it, and Mr. Davis would not be publicly humiliated.

The record does not conclusively support any of these possible interpretations. But we have to guess because motive so colors how the comments were made and so, finally, what those comments were, what "message" they were meant to convey. *We always do this when we read.* And we should always do it when we write. The meta-signals are often more significant than the surface ones.

And what do we learn about Harvey Davis from his

response? Especially about Harvey Davis *as a manager*? A lot, and all of it bad. The bottom line is that he loses an excellent employee. Excellent employees are hard to find these days; excellent geologists willing to work for government wages, I would bet, even harder. After you cool down, you *read the revisions* that Anonymous contributed. You then find out who Anon. is and call him or her in for a confidential chat. Maybe you'll learn something else valuable about how your prose is being received in the office. Even tactless Anon. may be able to teach you some lessons in tone. And that's that. No lawsuit, no job to fill, no big fuss. Instead, Harvey's egotism forces him to publicize him humiliation. Parade his bad prose style.

And the prose style wasn't even his! "In January 1978, Mr. Davis circulated a memorandum over his signature to his division directors within the agency. The memo had actually been prepared by a staff attorney." Harvey feels not the wrath of a prose style scorned but *lese majesty*. The revisor has attacked not his prose but his position, his self-esteem. Like a medieval baron, he rages because someone has dared to strike his servant. The memo itself becomes simply a pawn in a power confrontation. The Court infers that Davis was "strained by the inevitable tensions consequent to his new position." Maybe so, but the real reason seems to be native insecurity and an ego the size of an elephant.

The writer's block, or writer's loathing maybe we should call it, which many business people feel, often comes not from lack of something to say, or even hesitation about how to say it, but from fear. Fear that their memo will encounter a Harvey Davis somewhere up the line. The persistent *euphemism* that pervades business writing—have you ever noticed all the circumlocutions for "money" in corporate discourse?—comes from a fear of giving offense. More often than not, the Official Style is pressed into service not to fool people or parade pomposity but as an act of *piety*. People want to do the right thing. They want, at whatever cost to prose style or efficient communication, to behave properly.

The Paramedic Method offers no help here. Only wide and attentive reading will let you command the whole tonal range of prose and only tact and a keen social sense will create a prose that gets the message across in a way that soothes your boss rather than rattling her cage. People never write in a vacuum. This little lesson in management—for it is bad management as much as bad prose that stands at issue here—shows that business writing always has to work in a power structure and always function, in one way or another, as an element of that structure. When the boss tells you to be clear, be careful. She may not want you to be *that* clear.

Now, what about the prose that set off this land mine? It is legal prose, a memo drafted by a lawyer, citing a legal document (the Texas Water Code), giving instructions about testimony in court. This kind of litigious environment pervades business and government today, as we all know. As a result, the language of the law becomes a major force in business writing, a twin pincer that, with the Official Style, threatens to squeeze plain English out of even the simplest document. Legal language is a study in itself, and we haven't time for it here. (The classic work on the subject, for those who are interested, is David Mellinkoff's brilliant *The Language of the Law*, Boston: Little, Brown, 1963.) But the pressure to *sound legalistic* even if you are not a lawyer or drafting a statute has become relentless in business today. Everyone is afraid of being sued and legal-sounding language seems the only flak-vest around.

Legal language at its worst has a lot in common with the Official Style. Look at the first sentence of the memo:

The position
   of the Executive Director
   is developed
   during application review
   by legal and technical staff and formalized
   prior to submission
   of the application and the recommendation

    of the Executive Director
    to the Commission
    for setting
    of a contested APA hearing.

Our standard Official Style formula. No focus. No rhythm. No emphasis. No voice. Hard to read. It is riddled with mistakes, as Ms. Macpherson points out, but misplaced modifiers and unidiomatic prepositions are not the main problems. It is the vices of the Official Style, the endless, shapeless, actionless shopping-bag sentences, which drag it down. Try a PM number on it. What comes out, finally, is some dangerous advice. Employees will tell the truth when under oath, of course, but once the position of the Executive Director has been decided upon "each representative is expected to advocate the position taken." This comes perilously close to counselling perjury, as Ms. Macpherson tries to point out in her closing comment: "It is obvious to me that when one is subpoenaed one must appear, regardless of the opinion of the Department. Furthermore, one must tell the truth when under oath." This kind of shrewd observation a good boss ignores at his peril, however impertinently it may be wrapped up. For it points out the central contradiction of the memo, one that could get Harvey Davis in serious legal trouble.

Legal language defends itself usually by arguing that it must sacrifice elegance on the altar of clarity. But here the style becomes so official that sense is completely obscured. The strategy of legal language as self-defense has boomeranged, left the Agency open to a legal peril it has created itself. If Ms. Macpherson had been able to wrap this point up in enough deference, perhaps Mr. Davis would have been able to see it and pass the criticism along to its real target, the staff attorney who wrote the memo in the first place.

Legal language need not confound itself in its own Official Style, of course. Just look at the splendid prose of Judge Gee's opinion. He does admit that he has paid attention to his prose:

"In anticipation of a critical review of our remarks, we have been at some pains with their style and grammar." But the authority of his prose comes from tone, not good grammar. He must first show us that he, too, can see what is wrong with the memo, but notice how easily and indirectly he does so. Ms. Macpherson had neglected to remark the unidiomatic preposition in the memo's title but the Judge does not; he simply puts a "[sic]" after it to mark the error without writing, as I did earlier, a song about it. He then comments on the memo: "Like the title, portions of it were poorly worded." He then makes plain the subtext of Ms. Macpherson's comments: "She . . . proceeded to correct Mr. Davis's memo in searching detail, appending both specific and general comments calculated to bring home to the author his literary ineptitude." He thus shows us that he can read both kinds of "content," establishes his credentials as a literary critic. At the same time, he is establishing his human judgment as well, his qualifications for his own job. From his tone flows his authority.

If Ms. Macpherson's prose revision stands disastrously at odds with its social context, the Judge's sense of style fits its context exactly. Look at the contrast between how Judge Gee describes what happened and the trial court's Official Style version:

> While adhering to the ceiling of his office, revised memo in hand, Mr. Davis determined to fire the reviser, whomever he or she might be.

The plain style, with an ironical allusion to the Official Style—"while adhering to the ceiling of his office"—that one might expect. Then the ever so slightly ironical introduction to the trial court's lumpen description:

> As the trial court chastely put it in Finding of Fact No. 16, "The termination decision was made prior to the discovery of the identity of the employee who revised the memo and anonymously sent it to Mr. Harvey Davis."

95

Judge Gee's language proves that he can both see a prose style and see through and around it. And the stylistic command is read as a judgmental command: he can read human behavior with equal skill and tact.

He also knows, rarest of all, how to write a short sentence. And even, look at this, how powerful a short sentence will become when it follows a long one:

> Since the decision to fire Ms. Macpherson was taken when her identity, and perforce her gender, were unknown and merely carried out after they were discovered, there can be no question of sex discrimination on this record. There it ends.

I've spent so much time on this sad and funny case because it points so directly and economically to the context in which prose revision always occurs, the boundary conditions within which the PM must be applied. Applying it may be laborious but it is not arcane. Anyone can do it. This kind of revision can be formulaic because the prose it seeks to revise is formulaic, too. But there is nothing formulaic about when and how, and why, we do it. To answer those questions we must leave the schoolroom and depend on such native wit and good sense as any of us is lucky enough to possess.

CHAPTER 6

Why Bother?

I've been arguing that much of our writing problem comes from the goals and attributes that make up the Official Style. We have seen what the Official Style looks like: dominantly a noun style; a concept style; a style whose sentences have no design, no shape, rhythm, or emphasis; an unreadable, voiceless, impersonal style; a style built on euphemism and various kinds of poetic diction; above all, a style with a formulaic structure, "is" plus a string of prepositional phrases before and after. But just because it *is* a formulaic style, we can use a formula to revise it into plain English. The Paramedic Method handles the problem nicely. We might usefully review it here:

1. Circle the prepositions.
2. Circle the "is" forms.
3. Ask "Who is kicking who?"
4. Put this "kicking" action in a simple (not compound) active verb).
5. Start fast—no mindless introductions.
6. Write out each sentence on a blank sheet of paper and mark off its basic rhythmic units with a "/".
7. Read the passage aloud with emphasis and feeling.
8. Mark off sentence lengths in the passage with a "/".

To repeat: This formula does work, but it works only because the style it aims to revise is so formulaic to begin with. It really is a *paramedic* method, an emergency procedure. Don't confuse it with the art of medicine, with knowing about the full range of English prose styles—how to recognize and how to write them. That kind of knowledge is what English composition is all about. We are talking here about a subdivision of that broader field, about only *one kind* of stylistic revision. Because it is only one kind, it leaves a lot out.

Most obviously, it leaves out time, place, and circumstance. It aims to be clear and brief, but often if the social surface is to be preserved, clarity and brevity must be measured out in small doses. We seldom communicate *only* neutral information; we are incorrigibly interested in the emotions and human relationships that go with it.

Because the Paramedic Method ignores this aspect of writing, it can get you into trouble. Well, then, you might well ask, "Why bother?" The kind of revision we've been doing is hard work. Why do it if it's only going to get us in trouble? Why sit in your office and feel foolish trying to read a memo aloud for rhythm and shape? If the Official Style is the accepted language of our bureaucratic world, why translate it into English? Why stand up when everyone else is sitting down? Questions to be asked, though to answer we'll have to go a step or two beyond paramedicine. There are two answers, really, or rather two kinds of answers—"efficiency" answers and "ego" answers.

"Efficiency" first. A reader of the earlier version of this book made the main point for me:

> "Why bother?" You omitted one of the most important reasons: Cost.
>
> Two years ago our new organization needed a Constitution and By-Laws, and a By-Laws Committee was appointed for the task. They found a sample from a similar organization, made title and other changes and produced the 12-page Constitution and By-Laws. That was not sufficient, however, and they were instructed to add more "management organization" to the Constitution. But then, of course, the By-Laws didn't agree with the ex-

panded Constitution. One By-Laws amendment corrected one disparity, but others remained. It appeared to me that when the By-Laws were expanded to match the expanded Constitution, 19 pages of that format would be required. It was getting out of hand, and the reproduction costs could break our meager treasury.

A few months ago a friend told me about *Revising Prose,* and suggested its principles might be applied to By-Laws as much as to straight prose. I was skeptical at first but I zeroed-in on Who's Kicking Who, eliminating useless words, nonsense phrases and needless repetition. And because we had never appointed all that added management organization, I simply eliminated them. The fever was catching, and I challenged myself to get it on four pages. To do that I used the left margin for headings and maximized print density by eliminating as much white area as possible. Our "lard factor" was perhaps as high as you've ever seen.

The result is our new-look Constitution and By-Laws with easily-located subjects, quicker to read with improved comprehension, and technically more accurate. One copy now costs 20¢ versus 60¢ in the original and 95¢ if we had culminated the expansions. At our most recent meeting on April 19, 1980, it was adopted unanimously with only one change: the part about Assessments was stricken completely because it had never been noticed before and, now that it was easy to see, the idea was unacceptable to the group!

A small instance for a large lesson. The cost—in money, time, perplexity—exacted by the Official Style is literally and metaphorically incalculable. If we could calculate it, though, it would certainly be the difference between 20 cents and 60 cents, and maybe between 20 cents and 95 cents. A two-thirds savings of time and money? A four-fifths saving? Whew! Imagine this kind of saving in a large corporation or government agency. These numbers may seem extravagant but the lard factor amounts to a deadly multiplier: my letter to you, two times as long as it needs to be, evokes a letter from you two times as long as mine and four times as long as the subject demands, and so on *ad infinitum*. In the context of this unforgiving multiplier, criteria like sentence shape, rhythm, and sound turn out to be less literary graces than cost-effective necessities. Reading aloud for rhythm may end up saving you money.

The reader's letter makes a second point as essential as the first—the backpressure that revision exerts on thought and imagination. Revising what we write constitutes a self-satire, a debate with ourselves. The Paramedic Method brings ideas out into the open, denies them the fulsome coloration of a special language. If the ideas are unacceptable, like the "Assessments" section of the By-Laws, we'll see this clearly. The Official Style encourages us to fool ourselves as well as other people, to believe in our own bureaucratic mysteries. The Paramedic Method puts our ideas back under real pressure. They can then develop and grow or—painful as this always is—find their way to the circular file. If translation into plain English reveals only painful banalities, it's back to the drafting board for fresh ideas. The great thing about the Paramedic Method is that it allows us to conduct this self-education *in private*.

We can, too, think of efficiency and writing in a slightly different, but not in the end less cost-effective, way. We live in an age of bureaucracy, of large and impersonal organizations, public and private. We're not likely to change this much. Size and impersonality seem unavoidable concomitants of the kind of global planning we'll increasingly have to do. But surely the task of language is to leaven rather than to echo this impersonality. It is a matter of efficiency as well as of humanity and aesthetic grace. We understand ideas better when they come, manifestly, from other human beings. That is simply the way human understanding evolved. It is people, finally, who act, not offices, or even officers.

The kind of translation into plain English we've been

talking about can exert another kind of counterforce, as well. The Official Style is unrelievedly *abstract* as well as impersonal, echoes the bureaucratic preoccupation with concepts and rules. The Paramedic Method reverses the flow of this current from *concepts* back toward *objects*. It constitutes a ritual reminder to keep our feet on the ground. Dr. Johnson replied to the idealist philosopher's argument that the world exists only in our mind by kicking a stone. The Paramedic Method does much the same kind of thing for us—who's kicking who? The natural gravity of large organizations pulls so strongly toward concepts and abstractions that we need a formulaic counter-ritual. The Paramedic Method provides a start in this direction.

The language of bureaucracy, then, needs a cybernetic circuit to keep its dominant impetus toward impersonality and conceptual generalization in check. It ought to supply *negative* feedback, not the positive reinforcement provided by the Official Style. Such a counterstatement is not only more attractive and more fun—it's more efficient.

The "Ego" answers to "Why bother?" come harder than the "Efficiency" arguments because they are so closely invested with questions of morality, sincerity, hypocrisy, and the presentation of self. We might begin to sketch this answer by confronting the temptation head on. Why do all of us moralize so readily about writing style? Writing is usually described in a moral vocabulary—"sincere," "open," "devious," "hypocritical"—but is this vocabulary justified? Why do so many people feel that bad writing threatens the foundations of civilization? And why, in fact, do we think "bad" the right word to use for it? Why are we seldom content just to call it "inefficient" and let it go at that? Why to "clarity" and "brevity" must we always add a discussion of "sincerity" as well?

Let's start where "sincerity" starts, with the primary ground for morality, the self. We may think of the self as both a dynamic and a static entity. It is *static* when we think of ourselves as having central, fixed selves independent of our

101

surroundings, an "I" we can remove from society without damage, a central self inside our head. But it becomes dynamic when we think of ourselves as actors playing social roles, a series of roles that vary with the social situations in which we find ourselves. Such a social self amounts to the sum of all the public roles we play. Our *complex* identity comes from the constant interplay of these two selves. Our *final* identity is usually a mixed one, few of us being completely the same in all situations or, conversely, social chameleons who change with every context. What allows the self to grow and develop is the free interplay between these two kinds of self, the central self "inside our head" and the social self "out there." If we were completely sincere we would always say exactly what we think—and cause social chaos. If we were always acting an appropriate role, we would be either professional actors or certifiably insane. Reality, for each of us, presents itself as constant oscillation between these two extremes of interior self and social role.

When we say that writing is sincere, we mean that somehow it has managed to express this complex oscillation, this complex self. It has caught the accent of a particular self, a particular mixture of the two selves. Sincerity can't point to any *specific* verbal configuration, of course, since sincerity varies as widely as man himself. The sincere writer has not said exactly what he felt in the first words that occur to him. That might produce a revolutionary tirade or "like-you-know" conversational babble. Nor has a sincere writer simply borrowed a fixed language, as when a bureaucrat writes in the Official Style. The "sincere" writer has managed to create a style which, like the social self, can become part of society, can work harmoniously in society and, at the same time, like the central self, can represent his unique selfhood. He holds his two selves in balance; this is what "authority" in writing really means.

What the act of writing involves for the writer is an integration of his self, a deliberate act of balancing its two component parts. It represents an act of socialization, and it is by repeated acts of such socialization that we become sociable beings, that we grow up. Thus, the act of writing models the presentation of self in society, constitutes a rehearsal for social reality. It is not simply a question of a pre-existent self making its message known to a pre-existent society. From the "Ego" point of view, it is not, initially, a question of message at all. Writing is a way to clarify, strengthen, and energize the self, to render individuality rich, full, and social. This does not mean writing that flows, as Terry Southern immortally put it, "right out of the old guts onto the goddamn paper." Just the opposite. Only by taking the position of the reader toward one's own prose, putting a reader's pressure on it, can the self be made to grow. Writing can, through such pressure, enhance and expand the self, allow it to try out new possibilities, tentative selves. We return here to the backpressure revision exerts. It stimulates not only the mind but the whole personality. We are not simply offering an idea but our personality as context for that idea. And just as revision makes our ideas grow and develop, it encourages us to see the different ways we can act in society, the alternative paths to socialize the self.

The moral ingredient in writing, then, works first not on the morality of the message but on the nature of the sender, on the complexity of the self. "Why bother?" To invigorate and enrich your selfhood, to increase, in the most literal sense, your self-consciousness. Writing, properly pursued, does not make you better. It makes you more alive, more coherent, more in control. A mind thinking, not a mind asleep. It aims, that is, not to denature the human relationship that writing sets up, but to enhance and enrich it. It is not trying to squeeze out the expression of personality but to make such expression possible, not trying to obscure all record of a particular occasion and its human relationships but to make them maximally clear. Again, this is why we worry so much about bad writing. It signifies incoherent people, failed social relationships. This worry makes sense only if we feel that writing, ideally, should express human relationships and feelings, not abolish them.

From the "Ego" point of view, then, we revise the Official

103

Style when it fails to socialize the self and hence to enrich it, to discipline the ego to the surrounding egos that give it meaning. This, unhappily, is most of the time. Pure candor can be soundly destructive but so can pure formula, endless cliché. When formula takes over, self and society depart. The joy goes out of the prose. It's no fun to write. And when this happens, you get those social gaffes, those trodden toes, those "failures of communication" that so often interfere with the world's business. The human feeling that has been pushed out the front door sneaks in the back. So when you cease to feel good about what you write, when you cease to add something of yourself to it, watch out!

When we try to put these two answers to "Why bother?" together, we discover a paradoxical convergence. Cases do exist where one answer will do by itself—in the By-Laws case, for example, the "Efficiency" argument really is all we need—but more often than not the two kinds of justification support one another. The "Efficiency" argument, pressed hard enough, comes to overlap the "Ego" argument and vice versa. We may, in this area of overlap, have come across the richness we feel when we use all the customary value-laden terms to describe a piece of prose—"sincere," "honest," "fresh," "straightforward," and so on. We feel that somehow ego and efficiency have come to collaborate in establishing a clarity that makes understanding a pleasure and a shared one.

At this point, the paramedic analogy breaks down. Beyond paramedicine lies medicine; beyond the specific analysis of a specific style—what we have been doing here—lies the study of style in general. Verbal style can no more be fully explained by a set of rules, stylistic or moral, than can any other kind of human behavior. Intuition, *trained* intuition, figures as strongly in the one as in the other. You must learn how to see.

You'll then be able to answer the fundamental question that this chapter—and this book—can only introduce. *How* to revise the Official Style is easy—a piece of cake. As we've seen, anyone can do it. The questions that generate no rules, the questions that try our judgment—and our goodness—are *when?* and *why?*

CHAPTER 7

A Note on the Electronic Word

As is often the case with a new technology, we don't yet have a word for the electronically-displayed word. It makes no sense to call it electronic "print," for the fixity of print is just what it abolishes. Whatever we come to call it, though, it is making an enormous difference in how we write and especially in how we revise. The greater ease in revision made possible by word processors has been widely noticed. They make it so much easier to get the words down (but not "on paper" or "in print"!), to take them up and move them around. And the speed with which revision takes place means, often, that more revision can take place when writing—as we usually do—under a deadline. No need to go through those one-day retyping turnarounds for each revision. All in all, users of the Paramedic Method have never had it so easy.

And some even deeper changes seem in store for us. The first, as anyone in business can now attest, must be an increasing use of graphics to convey information. Although often "printed out," almost all graphic information is computer-generated at some point. The whole relationship of verbal and visual communication is changing. Now this usually means a more frequent use of the piecharts and bar graphs we have known for a long time. But in the future, we'll come to some closer overlaps between visual and verbal mediums. We are so used to the convention of print—linear, regular left-to-right and top-to-bottom, black-and-white, constant font and type size—that we have forgotten how constraining it is. It is remarkable not only for its power in expressing conceptual thought but for all the powers it renounces in doing so. No pictures, no color, no perspective. Up to now these things have been just too expensive. No longer. On the electronic screen, you can do them all and a lot more. And as electronic memory gets ever cheaper, they will come within the reach not only of graphics designers but of us everyday wordsmiths as well.

The constraints of conventionally-printed prose will slowly dissolve. If we can use color, font size and shape, three-dimensional effects like drop-shadow and the like, then we will use them. If we can intersperse text and graphics with ease, we'll come to depend on the combination. All these changes will, in their turn, change how we write and indeed how we think. The black-and-white letters-only convention concentrates on abstract thought—the "meaning"—to the exclusion of everything else. Tonal colorations there will always be—they are what we usually call "style"—but in print they are always beneath the surface, implicit rather than explicit. As we have seen in the Macpherson case, bringing them to the surface takes a lot of time and trouble. With the electronic word, however, these tonal colorations will be explicit rather than implicit. We will be able, literally, to "color" our communications with one another. And there will be no going back, no abjuration of this new realm of communication. If you can write "in color," and choose not to, that too will be a "communication," and usually one you will not want to make. So don't be fooled by that black and white—or, in the case of these words, green and white—screen. How often nowadays do you watch black and white TV? And what does it seem like when you do?

When we write we inevitably adopt a social role of some sort. Trying to bring this presentation of self to self-consciousness has been one of our main tasks in this book. The kind of self we will adopt in computer communication, especially on-line and, to a lesser degree in electronic mail, will differ from the "print" self. I'm not altogether sure why this is so but it does seem to be so. For reasons I will leave to the psychologists, computers have from their beginnings evoked the game and play ranges of human motivation far more strongly than print. The whole "hacker" personality that created the computer was suffused with the competition game impulse, but equally with the "for-its-own-sake" impulse just to do something to see if it could be done. Those of us struggling after the pioneers lie a far way off from this hacker mentality, but some of it seems inevitably to rub off when we put our fingers on the home row. We hold language more lightly in our hands; our sense of humor stands closer. All the better, I would say, for avoiding the Official Style and its systematic pomposity. The "dignity of print" has a lot to answer for. Let's hope that the electronic word preserves the muse of comedy that has hovered around its creation. At all events, it is something to watch for if you are writing and revising business prose in an "electronic" office.

The business press is full of predictions these days about the changes that an "information society" will bring. Let me end with one that emerges from our labors at prose revision. The logic of a society built on information instead of, or in addition to, goods, will lead us to a self-consciousness about words and the signals they broadcast far greater than now customary in the business world. The kind of verbal self-consciousness that now seems restricted to writers and literary critics will, by the very technological "logic" of an electronic information society, become a central management skill. "Business English" has always been an artificial category, an attempt to fabricate a special sublanguage for a spirit of commerce that ranges as wide as the world and needs the widest range of language in which to do business. Business in an information society will no longer be able to do business in "Business English." It will need "English" of every sort—and lots of other languages besides. That new conception of business prose—as wide as language itself, and as bright and sparkling as the electronic word can make it—promises a new and lively path whose ending none of us can foresee.

Terms

You can see things you don't know the names for but in prose style, as in everything else, it is easier to see what you know how to describe. The psychological ease that comes from calling things by their proper names has been much neglected in such writing instruction as still takes place. As a result, inexperienced writers often find themselves reduced to talking about "smoothness," "flow," and other meaningless generalities when they are confronted by a text. And so here are some basic terms.

Parts of Speech

In traditional English grammar, there are eight parts of speech: verbs, nouns, pronouns, adjectives, adverbs, prepositions, conjunctions, interjections. *Grammar,* in its most general sense, refers to all the rules that govern how meaningful statements can be made in any language. *Syntax* refers to sentence structure, to word order. *Diction* means simply word choice. *Usage* means linguistic custom.

Verbs

1. Verbs have two voices, active and passive.

An *active verb* indicates the subject acting:
Jack *kicks* Bill.

A *passive verb* indicates the subject acted upon:
Bill *is kicked* by Jim.

2. Verbs come in three moods: indicative, subjunctive, and imperative.

   A verb in the *indicative mood* says that something is a fact. If it asks a question, it is a question about a fact:

   > Jim *kicks* Bill. *Has* Jim *kicked* Bill yet?

   A verb in the *subjunctive mood* says that something is a wish or thought rather than a fact:

   > If Jim *were* clever, he *would* kick Bill.

   A verb in the *imperative mood* issues a command:

   > Jim, *kick* Bill!

3. A verb can be either *transitive* or *intransitive*.

   A *transitive verb* takes a direct object:

   > Jim kicks *Bill*.

   An *intransitive verb* does not take a direct object. It represents action without a specific goal:

   > Jim *runs* with great gusto.

   The verb "to be" ("is," "was," and so on) is often a *linking verb* because it links subject and predicate without transmitting a specific action:

   > Jim *is* a skunk.

4. English verbs have six tenses: present, past, present perfect, past perfect, future, and future perfect.

   > Present: Jim *kicks* Bill. (Present progressive: Jim *is kicking* Bill.)
   > Past: Jim *kicked* Bill.
   > Present perfect: Jim *has kicked* Bill.
   > Past perfect: Jim *had kicked* Bill.
   > Future: Jim *will kick* Bill.
   > Future perfect: Jim *will have kicked* Bill.

   The present perfect, past perfect, and future perfect are called *compound tenses*.

5. Verbs in English have three so-called *infinitive forms: infinitive, participle,* and *gerund.* These verb forms often function as adjectives or nouns.

Infinitive: To *kick* Jim makes great sport. ("To kick" is here the subject of "makes.")

Participles and gerunds have the same form; where the form is used as an adjective, it is called a *participle,* when used as a noun, a *gerund.*

Participles. Present participle: Jim is in a truly *kicking* mood. Past participle: Bill was a very well-*kicked* fellow.

Gerund: Kicking Bill is an activity hugely enjoyed by Jim.

(When a word separates the "to" in an infinitive from its complementary form, as in "to directly stimulate" instead of "to stimulate," the infinitive is said to be a *split infinitive.* Most people think this ought not to be done unless absolutely necessary.)

Verbs that take "it" or "there" as subjects are said to be in an *impersonal construction,* e.g., "It has been decided to fire him" or "There has been a personnel readjustment."

Nouns

A noun names something or somebody. A proper noun names a particular being—Jim.

1. *Number.* The singular number refers to one ("a cat"), plural to more than one ("five cats").
2. *Collective nouns.* Groups may be thought of as a single unit, as in "the army."

Pronouns

A pronoun is a word used instead of a noun. There are different kinds:

1. *Personal pronouns*—e.g., I, me, you, he, him, them.
2. *Intensive pronouns*—e.g., myself, yourself, himself.
3. *Relative pronouns*—e.g., who, which, that. These must have *antecedents,* words they refer back to. "Jim has a talent (antecedent) that (relative pronoun) Bill does not possess."
4. *Indefinite pronouns*—e.g., somebody, anybody, anything.
5. *Interrogative pronouns*—e.g., who?, what?

Possessives

Singular: A worker's hat. *Plural:* The workers' hats. ("It's," however, equals "it is." The possessive is "its.")

Adjectives

An *adjective* modifies a noun, e.g., "Jim was a *good* hiker."

Adverbs

An *adverb* modifies a verb, e.g., "Jim kicked *swiftly*."

Prepositions

A *preposition* connects a noun or pronoun with a verb, an adjective, or another pronoun, e.g., "I ran *into* her arms" or "The girl *with* the blue scarf."

Conjunctions

Conjunctions join sentences or parts of them. There are two kinds, coordinating and subordinating.

1. *Coordinating conjunctions*—e.g., and, but, or, for—connect statements of equal status, e.g., "Bill ran and Jim fell" or "I got up but soon fell down."
2. *Subordinating conjunctions*—e.g., that, who, when—connect a main clause with a subordinate one, e.g., "I thought *that* he had gone."

Interjection

A sudden outcry, e.g., "Wow!"

Sentences

Every sentence must have both a subject and verb, stated or implied, e.g., "Jim (subject) kicks (verb)."

Three Kinds

1. A *declarative sentence* states a fact, e.g., "Jim kicks Bill."
2. An *interrogative sentence* asks a question, e.g., "Did Jim kick Bill?"

112

3. An *exclamatory sentence* registers an exclamation, e.g., "Like, I mean, you know, like wow!"

Three Basic Structures

1. A *simple sentence* makes one self-standing assertion, i.e., has one main clause, e.g., "Jim kicks Bill."

2. A *compound sentence* makes two or more self-standing assertions, i.e., has two main clauses, e.g., "Jim kicks Bill and Bill feels it" or "Jim kicks Bill and Bill feels it and Bill kicks back."

3. A *complex sentence* makes one self-standing assertion and one or more dependent assertions, subordinate clauses, dependent on the main clause, e.g., "Jim, who has been kicking Bill these twenty-five years, kicks him still and, what's more, still enjoys it."

In *compound sentences,* the clauses are connected by *coordinating conjunctions,* in *complex sentences* by *subordinating conjunctions.*

Restrictive and Nonrestrictive Relative Clauses

A restrictive clause modifies directly, and so restricts the meaning of the antecedent it refers back to, e.g., "This is the tire *that blew out on the freeway.*" One specific tire is intended. In such clauses the relative clause is *not* set off by a comma.

A nonrestrictive clause, though still a dependent clause, does not directly modify its antecedent and is set off by commas. "These tires, which are quite expensive, last a very long time."

Appositives

An *appositive* is an amplifying word or phrase placed next to the term it refers to and set off by commas, e.g., "Henry VIII, *a glutton for punishment,* had six wives."

Noun Style and Verb Style

Every sentence must have a noun and a verb, but one can be emphasized, sometimes almost to the exclusion of the other.

113

The Official Style—strings of prepositional phrases and "is"—exemplifies a noun style *par excellence*. Here are three examples, the first of a noun style, the second of a verb style, and the third of a balanced noun-verb mixture.

NOUN STYLE

There is in turn a two-fold structure of this "binding-in." In the first place, by virtue of internalization of the standard, conformity with it tends to be of personal, expressive and/or instrumental significance to ego. In the second place, the structuring of the reactions of alter to ego's action as sanctions is a function of his conformity with the standard. Therefore conformity as a direct mode of the fulfillment of his own need-dispositions tends to coincide with the conformity as a condition of eliciting the favorable and avoiding the unfavorable reactions of others.

(Talcott Parsons, *The Social System* [Glencoe, Ill.: Free Press, 1951], p. 38)

VERB STYLE

Patrols, sweeps, missions, search and destroy. It continued every day as if part of sunlight itself. I went to the colonel's briefings every day. He explained how effectively we were keeping the enemy off balance, not allowing them to move in, set up mortar sites, and gather for attack. He didn't seem to hate them. They were to him like pests or insects that had to be kept away. It seemed that one important purpose of patrols was just for them to take place, to happen, to exist; there had to be patrols. It gave the men something to do. Find the enemy, make contact, kill, be killed, and return. Trap, block, hold. In the first five days, I lost six corpsmen—two killed, four wounded.

(John A. Parrish, *12, 20 & 5: A Doctor's Year in Vietnam* [Baltimore: Penguin Books, 1973], p. 235)

MIXED NOUN-VERB STYLE

We know both too much and too little about Louis XIV ever to succeed in capturing the whole man. In externals,

in the mere business of eating, drinking, and dressing, in
the outward routine of what he loved to call the *metier du
roi*, no historical character, not even Johnson or Pepys, is
better known to us; we can even, with the aid of his own
writings, penetrate a little of the majestic facade which is
Le Grand Roi. But when we have done so, we see as in a
glass darkly. Hence the extraordinary number and variety
of judgments which have been passed upon him; to one
school, he is incomparably the ablest ruler in modern
European history; to another, a mediocre blunderer, pompous, led by the nose by a succession of generals and civil
servants; whilst to a third, he is no great king, but still the
finest actor of royalty the world has ever seen.

(W. H. Lewis, *The Splendid Century: Life in the France of Louis XIV* [N.Y.:
Anchor Books, 1953], p. 1)

For further explanation of the basic terms of grammar, see
George O. Curme's *English Grammar* in the Barnes & Noble
College Outline Series.